# Preaching in a New Key

# Preaching in a New Key

## Studies in the Psychology of Thinking and Listening

**Clement Welsh**

**A PILGRIM PRESS BOOK**
from United Church Press,
Philadelphia

Library of Congress Cataloging in Publication Data

Welsh, Clement, 1913–
   Preaching in a new key: Studies in the psychology
of thinking and listening.

   "A Pilgrim Press book."
   Includes bibliographical references.
   1. Preaching.   2. Perception.   3. Cognition.
I. Title.
BV4211.2.W42      251      74–5268
ISBN 0–8298–0273–8

United Church Press, 1505 Race Street,
Philadelphia, Pennsylvania 19102

For my wife,
who transposed my life into a new key,
added a melodic voice,
and over the years
produced a harmonious chorus
in our home

# Contents

# Preface

This essay began as a series of explorations designed to find out what goes on in the mind of anyone listening to a sermon. They were addressed at first to many patient people attending conferences at the College of Preachers in Washington, D.C. An invitation to give the Bradner Lectures at the Episcopal Theological School in Cambridge, Massachusetts, provided an opportunity to give these reflections a more formal shape, now in these pages enlarged and annotated.

But "explorations" they remain. Even arranged in chapter form, they may be thought of as forming an extended introduction to a book not yet written, the substance of which may be indicated by the studies referred to in the notes. They are concerned with the listener as one who makes sense of his universe, and since it is the listener rather than the preacher who is the center of attention,

9

much of the usual material relevant to a study of preaching is left out. Questions concerning orthodoxy of content, or concerning the problem of how to present the Divine Word in human words, or concerning the arts of presentation—these, and other prescribed topics for works on homiletics, are chapters in other books, and a surfeit of them is readily available.

There are, however, chapters that ought to have been written and are omitted with regret. The mind defies summary treatment, and these explorations are summary indeed, leaving important areas unvisited, such as the extensions of consciousness, the springs of creativity, and the upper reaches of the imagination. The explorations have just begun.

The Lester Bradner Lectures, established by the children of Lester Bradner (1876–1929), are shared by the Episcopal Theological School, Cambridge, Massachusetts, the Protestant Episcopal Theological Seminary in Virginia, and the General Theological Seminary, New York. The lectures presented here were delivered in Cambridge in December 1971, and the author is greatly indebted to the dean, the trustees, and faculty of the school for their hospitality, and to the trustees of the Lester Bradner Lectureship for the honor of being invited to give the lectures.

*1*

# On Receiving Messages from the Universe

I begin in an appropriate state of anxiety, for I intend to hold forth page after page on that most unlikely of subjects: preaching. If there can be anything deadlier than a sermon, it must be a discussion of sermons, a sermon on sermons.

Yet it is just this strange, dull, persistent, anachronistic action that illuminates an odd, rather baffling aspect of our life as a people. The sermon as an *event* may be, to speak with restraint, uneventful, but as a *symptom* it yields on analysis unsuspectedly rich information about the state of our minds. The demonstration of this will be the theme of the pages to come, but at least a preliminary justification of the thesis can be put this way, that at the time of the sermon the vast majority of the people in our particular corner of Western civilization encounter their only systematic exposure to any kind of reflection on the meaning of things. More people hear sermons than read editorials, attend plays, or discuss B. F. Skinner. Our general metaphysical state of mind may be exposed by a study of preaching, for it is a cultural event that reveals the working of those mysterious forces that shape values and determine presuppositions.

For the sermon is at once popular and profound. The preacher tries to probe the depths, but with only the tools that are handy. He takes the flower in the crannied wall and urges us toward an awareness of its eternal meaning, sometimes by way of Karl Barth, John Calvin, Augustine, Paul, and a parable from Luke's gospel; it is a long ladder to ascend, and not everyone makes it to the top.

The themes of the sermon range from the common immediacies of daily issues to deeper and more abstract presuppositions about life, some of them consciously brought to the surface, some of them hidden but active, shaping the imagination from below. Like a great lens, the sermon draws light from many sources and tries to bring it to a focus, happily as an illumination upon some matter of current concern.

Although the sermon may be described as an isolated event (reported at Sunday dinner by those who heard it in an effort to edify those who stayed away) it can best be understood as an element in a *system*, and as related to other systems. It occurs almost without exception within the context of a sacred rite, a liturgy, which means that it is carefully orchestrated as a part of a complex structure. It has a *place* (pulpit), an appropriate *time-length*, and in many liturgies, a proper *time-position*. The actors who engage in the sermon have their traditional parts, places, and behavior, all related to the institutional context of the event. Few public actions are so carefully set within a defined network of interlocked procedures.

Yet the sermon is not just one thing systematically related to other things, other systems. It is also an art form, which means that it has an internal system of fantastic complexity. Its internal elements comprise a system which, one hopes, is under the control of its creator, and which is designed to have its own unity, form, and theme. Its form, like its cognitive content, reverberates in various ways with that larger aesthetic system that is now often discussed under the heading of *media*. The sermon as a medium of communication requires our special attention, for if cognitive content (values and metaphysics) ranks low in our culture, aesthetic form (media and style) ranks high. As a people we may not have much to say that is enlightening, but we can say it with the speed of light, and to millions.

These elements of the larger system are visible, and operate almost automatically. More subtle interrelationships, less visible, are equally important. For the sermon is a *cognitive event* as well as an experienced action (it is experienced, and therefore more than just cognitive, for it taps emotions, the subconscious, and other human behaviors). As a cognitive event, the sermon functions as part of a vast and diffuse system, *the belief-disbelief system* of a particular time and place. Both preacher and listener share in this system, in as many ways as there are warm bodies present, and we shall be interested in the differences among them and in the similarities. As a *congregation* (such as a group of blue-collar Methodists in Akron, Ohio) they exemplify a belief system held in common; that's one of the reasons they get together. But they share with the Polish Roman Catholics nearby, and even with the sleeping agnostics who have not yet awakened to read the Sunday

13

comics, a larger belief system: an American twentieth-century version of Western European Judaeo-Christian culture, which is a very muddied river indeed, fed by many alien streams, and running rather dry these days.

We are a people confronted by massive shifts and changes in the value system that we had been taking for granted. That has been an unsettling experience, and to make it worse, the changes are occurring in an area of life where we have never operated easily; indeed, who ever has? Philosophy has never really been the American thing, except for Transcendentalism, Pragmatism, and its relatives. This situation gives new responsibilities to preaching, for we recognize that the sermon is one place, at least, where our rather nonmetaphysical culture can legitimately expect such matters as values to be dealt with. Since a nation can neglect all the standard topics of an introductory course in philosophy just so long, a place that provides public and frequent reflection on first principles becomes a place of national importance. Just those matters which higher education has not handled very well in recent years are the ones that the sermon takes as its primary business, and the preacher conducts today what may be as strange a system of adult education as any culture has ever tried. It is an astonishing effort at groundroots metaphysics, and to borrow Johnson's male chauvinist comment on women preaching—it is not surprising that it is done badly, but surprising, rather, that it is done at all, especially in what we are told is an individualistic, sensuous, materialistic, cynical, and anti-intellectual society. All the more surprising that since it is indeed done badly, it nevertheless *continues* to be done.

It is the interaction of these various systems that will involve us in that rather new, interdisciplinary set of studies called, "human communication theory." [1] For what holds these subsystems together into a larger system, operating constantly in both open and hidden ways, *is the transfer of information.* All the systems are communication systems. A system is maintained within itself and is kept in rapport with other systems by the movement of information within it. The body of a system is its structure, but communication is its soul. One could define a system as a communications complex maintained by the circulation within it of appropriate information: genetic, neural, linguistic, symbolic, the language that is common to the system. As a communication event, the sermon attempts to form a homiletical system from several existing systems, weaving together into a new supersystem the loose systems of ideas and feelings that form the religious heritage and the several secular systems operating within the culture.

The focal point of all this is the listener, each individual person who is the central point of the intricate cobweb of lines of influence and concern that make up a fragile life. As he sits before the preacher, he could be considered, not too mechanically I hope, the most fantastic processor of information that the world has ever seen, weaving into some sort of personal pattern the inputs from his age, his country, his work, his family, his friends, and from a hundred sources of packaged information, and shaping all this with the help of experiences and learnings too various to list. He survives and grows by processing the information received from his environment. He observes, remembers, reflects, imagines, and makes sense of his universe.

The preacher, standing in his special place, looks across at this processing creature and asks the complex question: "What shall I do to help him grow? How shall I enable him to perceive, to understand, and to act: to do the human thing with the aid of those who have been most human before him?" As a preacher, his function is not "to communicate." His function is to enable the listener to communicate with his universe; that is, to receive the bombardment of data from his world and to make useful sense of it. For this process is the distinctively human work, beginning with our first sensory responses to our environment, and continuing on to metaphysics, and for which we are given the extraordinary instrument we call the mind.

The preacher enters this process at a very high level. Or, to reverse the metaphor, at the level of depth. His function is partly therapeutic, partly educational. He does not drop a "message" into a box made ready for it. He hopes to adjust, delicately, some elements of the receiving mechanism to help it function more adequately. Like any good teacher or therapist, he hopes to make himself dispensable.

This is our theme, this is our purpose in these pages: to work out a theory of preaching that takes seriously a person as a center where messages from a universe are received and dealt with, and which is based on an analysis of a person as one who does that, unlikely though it may at first sound. It is an approach that draws upon whatever we can find out about man as a processor of information, and at the same time it keeps an ear cocked to those who cry out, with a certain proper irritation, "But man is more than this!"

And to begin, we drop back twenty-five years, and observe the emergence of an analytical tool that we propose to use.

# 2

# From Source to Destination

The year is 1948. In that year, in a magazine with the unheroic title *The Bell System Technical Journal,* an article was published by Claude Shannon on "A Mathematical Theory of Communication." In the same year a second publication appeared: *Cybernetics: or Control and Communication in the Animal and in the Machine,* by Norbert Wiener.[1] Probably far more people noticed Wiener's book than Shannon's article, but in retrospect either publication could make the year memorable, and taken together they mark the coming of age of important ideas. If an era was not born in 1948, at least it achieved then a new degree of self-awareness, and several names, and we can take one of them as a convenient label: 1948 inaugurates the serious study of "communication."

But even as we say that we are in trouble. Clearly the study of communication did not begin in 1948. It might be maintained that it began in Eden, when Adam named the animals (and reaching, perhaps, a crisis of research at the Tower of Babel). And the word communication can seem paradoxically self-defeating. It has an unpleasantly dull sound, like a cracked bell, seeming to deny by its own sound its very sense, or to be a pedantic way of avoiding shorter and better terms like "speech" or "talk." As a word, "communication" does not communicate.

Yet the word has been formalized and has become the label for a box full of strange things. All sorts of special meanings have been crowded into it. It might have been better to have invented a new word, one which would warn everyone by its novelty that it is intended to point to an arbitrary collection of data. This was, in fact, what Norbert Wiener intended to do with the word cybernetics.

> Cybernetics is a word invented to define a new field in science. It combines under one heading the study of what in a human context is sometimes loosely described as thinking and in engineering is known as control and communication. In other words, cybernetics attempts to find the common elements in the functioning of automatic machines and of the human nervous system, and to develop a theory which will cover the entire field of control and communication in machines and in living organisms.[2]

Wiener derived the word from the Greek word for steersman (κυβερνήτης) discovering later that it had been used in 1934 by Ampere in his *Essai sur la Philosophie des Sciences*, and that the Latin cognate, "governor," had been used by James Clark Maxwell to designate the familiar control mechanism.

Nevertheless, in contrast to "pragmatism," described by William James as "a new word for some old ways of thinking," [3] it was the fate of "communication" to become an old word for many new ways of thinking. "Communication theory," concerning the transfer of "information," combines a mathematical theory with the practical needs that Shannon faced in dealing with matters of electrical communication. The problems he was dealing with were engineering problems, and they had engaged scientists for some years. Since we are more likely to know the history of the Civil War than we are of the development of science, a rapid listing of a few major achievements in electrical communication may be helpful. As early as 1746, Sir William Watson had sent a current of electricity over 10,600 feet of wire, and a few years later an anonymous writer in *Scots Magazine* suggested a telegraph system using one wire for each letter. Various double or multiwire systems were tried, but it was Samuel F. B. Morse who demonstrated in 1838 to the President and his Cabinet, a workable system extending over the forty miles between Baltimore and Washington, and with that formal success, and the establishment of a commercial system over that distance in 1844, telegraphy was on its way. The origins of the telephone with Alexander Graham Bell and his first successful message to Mr. Watson are now a part of technology's folklore. The growth of the use of telephones began slowly but expanded rapidly. In 1880, there were 47,000 telephones in use; in 1890, 227,000; in 1900, there were 1,355,000; in 1910, there were 7,635,400; and in 1920, 13,329,400. Radio and television are twentieth-century achievements.

By 1922, when *The Bell System Technical Journal* was founded, the demands on electrical communication equipment were mounting. What was needed was an understanding of the capacity of electrical channels to take messages: how many, how clearly, how cheaply. Shannon was working within a growing body of theoretical work which was not only English and American, but international; important contributions came, for example, from Germany by Küpfmüller and from Russia by Kolmogoroff.

A significant aspect of this work is the way it seemed applicable not only to the problems of message transmission electrically for which it was intended, but also to any kind of communication. In the foreword to the first issue of the *Journal* it was said, "A casual examination of recent technical literature dealing with electrical communication would show articles which touch upon almost every branch of human activity which we designate as science." The first volume of the *Journal* included articles illustrative of such outward reaching. "The Nature of Speech and Its Interpretation" was one, and "Physical Characteristics and Dynamic Analysis of the External Ear" was another.

In the creative period between 1928, the date of an important article by R. V. L. Hartley on "The Transmission of Information," and Shannon's article ("The Mathematical Theory of Information") in 1948, the words communication and information took on special meanings, leading inevitably to confusion with the general meanings of the words.

As a mathematical theory, the work of "information theory" was of great generality, and the details concerning it need not detain us, but it must be noted that the old word information is used with a special meaning referring to the measurement of messages and not to their semantic content.[4] Nevertheless, communication studies spread as a special approach to many academic disciplines. The basic mathematical ideas of information theory proved applicable to many processes in nature. Like the spreading of the idea of "evolution" into many fields of study after Darwin, the ideas of information theory were taken up rapidly after the publications of Shannon and Wiener. A study has been made of the first actual citations in academic literature of Wiener's book and of Shannon's article (or of its reprinting in 1949 with an explanatory essay by Warren Weaver).[5] Like an exfoliation of a family tree from two ancestors the bibliographical progeny can be traced.

It begins with psychiatry, in an article by Warren McCulloch on "The Brain as a Computing Machine" in 1949; in the same year, in an article that was to be widely influential, F. C. Frick and G. A. Miller added to the statistical study of biology the insights of information theory in their article, "Statistical Behavioristics and Sequences of Responses." H. Jacobson, in 1950, developed the ideas of Shannon for a study in physiology: "The Informational Capacity of the Human Ear," and in the next year reported similar studies of the eye. In 1950, N. Rashevsky published "Some Bio-sociological Aspects of the Mathematical Theory of Communication." Otto Straus considered its use in linguistics in "The Relation of Phonetics and Linguistics to Communication Theory" and Dennis Gabor reviewed its value to physics in "Communication Theory and Physics," both in 1950. In 1951, Wilbur Schramm brought together two lines of study, divergent in origin but now interrelated, in "Information Theory and Mass Communication."

R. L. Dahling, who made the study of the spreading influence of the papers by Shannon and Wiener, notes the importance of academic centers and interdisciplinary conferences for the growing excitement about information theory. Louis Ridenour at the University of Illinois showed the Shannon article to Wilbur Schramm, who was in charge of the university press, and suggested that Warren Weaver do an exposition of the Shannon article and that they be published together. Ridenour, Schramm, and the Library School at the university then arranged a symposium on the use of information theory in library science, and in 1951, the papers of the symposium were published as *Bibliography in an Age of Science.*[6]

Henry Quastler, a physician and radiologist, returned to the university at about that time and directed a symposium published as *Information Theory in Biology.*[7] Charles Osgood and George Miller had been working on the possibilities of the theory of information for linguistics, and Miller came to the University of Illinois to lecture. They arranged a symposium in 1954, and the papers, edited by Quastler, were published as *Information Theory in Psychology.*[8] In 1953, the University of Indiana had held a symposium on psycholinguistics, and Osgood, with T. A. Sebrock, published a report of its work as *Psycholinguistics: A Survey of Theory and Practice,* incorporating information theory.[9]

It was in 1955 that Wilbur Schramm specifically related the Shannon model of the communication process to the study of mass communication. Research in mass communication had had a long history, ranging all the way from basic psychological studies of interpersonal and social relationships to studies focused on the specific functioning of various kinds of communication media, such as the public press.[10] Within these studies of what seems more obviously to be "communication" and the transfer of "information" in the commonly accepted meanings of those words, the decades since World War II have produced a drawing together of what have often been isolated and diverse fields: small group behavior, propaganda, public speaking, personnel management, as well as mass media. To the commonly accepted idea of "organism," and its metaphorical applications outside the realms of biology, we may now add the concepts of the various forms of communication theory, with its mathematical information theory, cybernetics and feedback ideas, and their related notions, as providing a fresh look at how organisms operate. With an almost religious enthusiasm Harley C. Shands has said:

> The present discussion has the purpose of suggesting that perhaps the most important movement now observable is that of the creation of a massive new discipline combining elements of existing approaches throughout the arts and sciences. This discipline threatens to make obsolete all previous theories in philosophy as it increasingly asserts its right to the status of a "meta-discipline" under which all others can be subsumed as special cases with particular goals and methods. The field is generally concerned with *communication,* but in a way which makes it different from epistemology, semantics, symbolism, lexicography, linguistics, and the host of other disciplines in which there are already well-defined careers and courses.[11]

Attempts have been made to give this new discipline a definition. Colin Cherry offers this one:

> Perhaps the simplest and broadest definition of the word "communication" is afforded by this statement: "It is that which links any organism together." Here "organism" may

mean two friends in conversation, newspapers and their reading public, a country and its postal service and telephone system. At another level it may refer to the nervous system of an animal, while at another it may relate to a civilization and its culture. When communication ceases, the organism breaks up.[12]

And to this brief list he could have added: the sermon within the worshiping body of religious people. Such a body is a complex organism indeed, with multiple communication channels operating both within it, and between it and its environment. Each of these organic entities that Colin Cherry mentioned works out its own subdefinition of "communication," one appropriate to its life and structures. So with the sermon; any communications approach to the sermon must respect what is unique to that activity, and avoid the temptation to locate it under some other, such as "mass communication," or public speaking, or drama, or anything else. Yet a truly creative concept brings to diverse activities an interpretive model that preserves uniqueness even as it sets it within a larger family of behaviors. Encouraged by the successes of the communications model in areas as different as brain functions and the management of a business office, we shall look for whatever illumination communication theory can bring to preaching, respectfully aware that that is a behavior that is rich and strange.

*3*

# *From Preacher to Listener*

A good place to begin is with Shannon's original model.[1] As a model it has an elegant clarity, and it is simple enough to be safe, for it will not seduce us into thinking that it plots the location of all significant details. Let us find in it a first schematic view of the main process.

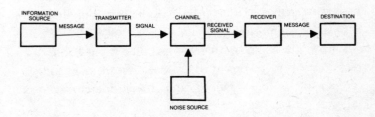

The model is easily read. An information source generates a message, and submits it to a transmitting process which codes it into a form which can be conveniently sent as a series of signals across a channel. The signals are received by a matching decoding element to reproduce from the received signal the original message, which is then available to the destination. Since Shannon was chiefly concerned with electronic communication, he was aware of the special importance of the channel and of its capacity to take many messages quickly and cheaply. Since no channel operates with absolute purity, a certain amount of noise is generated within it, and this joins the transmitted signal and is received at the destination. Thus the signal-to-noise ratio becomes important; too much noise can obscure the signal. If the signal contains "redundancy" (such as repetitions and clarifications, or highly probable elements) the receiver and destination can tolerate a high signal-to-noise ratio. "One if by land or two if by sea," however, is a message that might easily be distorted by faults in the system.

Shannon's basic model has received extensive enlargements by those who are working with human communication, as indeed it must for any application.[2] A glance at the interior of a television set suggests that the term "receiver" is pretty far from being an adequate description of what is there. Yet even in its simple form it can help to begin the process of analysis. Let us make with its help a preliminary analysis of the preaching event.

One might begin by saying, with some justification, that the situation to be described is "the preacher delivering a sermon to the congregation," and arrange the elements as follows:

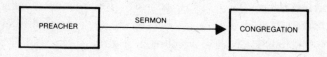

The Shannon diagram asks us to make important distinctions. Within the preacher, it says, are at least two separable functions: his origination of the message, and his formation of it into communicable form. Furthermore, within the congregation, each listener must exercise at least two separable functions: receiving the message and assimilating it. The delivery of the sermon functions as channel, usually by voice and by nonverbal behavior on the part of the preacher. From the point of view of the listener, other sounds and sights also are received, so the channel is infected by noise, with which the sermon must compete. When an elderly parishioner in the front row snores loudly, the signal-to-noise ratio can be disastrous for message transmission.

As in most, if not all, human communication, feedback also occurs, following the Shannon pattern, but this time from listener (alone and as a member of the group) to preacher; snoring would act as feedback as well as noise. Indeed, for human communication, all noise is in some sense message, as we shall see.

We can now adapt the Shannon model for preaching, still keeping the elements as simple as possible:

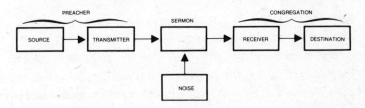

Even within this simple schematic representation, important elaborations are possible. Consider, if only as a preparation of an outline for future analysis, the preacher in his two functions: as source and as transmitter.

As *source,* the preacher may be considered as the point of connection between two systems. He is related in a special way to the congregation, as the authoritative person who has the right to speak. But he is also related to a larger system, which is partly institutional, and which gave him his professional credentials but which is also an intellectual and spiritual system related to him by various forms of cultural inputs and given to him, many would say, more directly by God (he brings God's "message," as the sermon is often termed). The preacher is also simply himself; standing there, even before he speaks, he is observed and known as a person, with varying degrees of admiration and trust. Evidently, an appropriate set of divisions must be made of the simple designation of preacher as "message source."

As *transmitter,* the preacher exercises both native communicative talents and the training he has received in various skills. His professional training supposedly includes such matters as the use of the voice and the art of shaping ideas into homiletical form, although a surprising number of preachers defeat themselves as soon as they start by mumbling and rambling. The major part of the transmitting function, however, is that of relating a massive and ancient heritage to contemporary life; as encoder, the preacher is plunged into some of the largest problems of contemporary Christianity. His concern, as he sets about the task of shaping the content of the sermon, ranges from problems in his sources (such as the validity of the Bible and the usefulness today of inherited theological teachings) to problems in his congregation (his understanding of their state of mind, and his reading of their personal and public problems). As he reflects on these, he must develop a strategy or intention, for not all things are possible, and not all things are advisable. As transmitter, with various coding options, the preacher has begun to reflect upon the listener as receiver, and upon his decoding abilities and his needs as the destination of the message. And like the preacher, the listener is a point of contact with other systems, some of them shared with the preacher, and some of them unique to the listener.

Linking these complex elements in the Shannon diagram is that innocent box marked "channel." Given the coding-decoding situation, and the decisions the preacher makes concerning it, what channel would be appropriate? Tradition has set the stage: pulpit (raised and remote) with silent congregation passively listening. Is this an appropriate medium? As medium does it contribute, as McLuhan has suggested, its own message, intruding at this point in the system an input that the preacher might consider noise?

Ominous questions can be raised about the sermon as a public verbal event without opportunity for feedback. But like every other element in the Shannon model, channel is a bundle of complexities. To focus attention only on technical matters, such as the delivery of a monologue from an isolated and elevated place, ignores what may be far more important, such as the context of the event, and the expectations of the participants. And discussions of "the validity of the sermon in an age of TV" may sound impressive, but sermons and TV operate in quite different communication systems; it is the system that determines the channel.

At the congregational end of the Shannon model, where the sermon is received and assimilated by the listener, the most important events of the whole system occur. To attempt to understand the receiving process will involve us in an extensive curriculum of subjects, of which the most salient have to do with the way any twentieth-century man reflects upon matters of ultimate significance when they are addressed to him. The preacher sends across to him a religious proposition which is a cognitive stimulus of great complexity. How competent is the receiver to process such a message? Into what sort of structural matrix does it intrude? Does it activate a kind of thinking for which the listener has little preparation? Does it stir up questions that the listener would rather leave undisturbed? For this process, in which a person is asked to plunge briefly to the level of first principles and brood there for twenty minutes, is one of the most difficult exercises a person can attempt. At the time of the sermon a person is asked to do an astonishing thing: begin making ultimate sense of everything. Yet most of us have trouble making partial sense of even a few things. When it comes to ultimates, we hope for a healthy tradition of prepared answers and of convenient symbolic shortcuts presented with authority and to which we can give thankful assent, joining in the chorus if someone else will sing the verses.

How much of this is simply human? How much is the result of living in a nonmetaphysical age? Granting that the religious commentators of every age deplore the contemporary atheism of their day, it seems evident that in our generation the receiving and decoding process of contemporary people, when the message is religious, operates with peculiar difficulty. Western Christian man shares with Western man the effects of "The Great Transition" to a "Post-Christian Mind," or even a "Post-Modern Mind." The use of the word mind in these analyses of cultural change is important; for some commentators, modern (or post-modern) man has a new "consciousness." Life in a technological world has shaped not only the content but also the functioning of our minds. We process perceptual data that is new, and the significant result is a change in the processing functions. Robert E. Mueller says:

> If we could take an adult Cro-Magnon man into the psychological laboratory, and compare him with a modern adult, he would no doubt be found to lack, most of all, sufficient perceptual sophistication to cope with modern reality. Any modern child would have an advantage over him, traceable to basic attitudes, words, concepts, images, and intrinsic art consciousness which had subliminally crept into his brain.[3]

The perceptual sophistication, the instinctive perceptual habits of a culture are learned only with difficulty, if at all, by anyone born and raised in a radically different culture. As McLuhan suggests, we need not go back to Cro-Magnon man to find a culture radically different from ours; the nineteenth century can provide it. As for the first four centuries of the Christian era, the implications of such analyses would be that the "mind" that produced the basic documents of the faith differed so much from ours that we are faced with far more than a problem of translation, of finding words to correspond with theirs. The important difference between ancient Christian statements and modern Christian ideas lies deeper, at the level of attitudes and values, and at that diffuse level of behavior where the decisions are made to observe or not to observe, to attend or not to attend.

In conformity with much conventional theological wisdom, then, we stress how extensive is the range of difficulties for the contemporary Christian when he must think about the faith and add: How many of these are presented in acute form by the preaching and hearing of sermons? For the sermon forces all concerned to move at cognitive levels and to draw upon presuppositions that tap an apparatus of metaphysics which is for most of us in a state of chronic disrepair even at the best of times.

We merely touch here on what will be a continuing theme of these pages. Preaching as an art form is brief and occasional. It must live or die by what it can presuppose and evoke. In our time, at the end of an age that has lived on borrowed ultimates, it often sounds like an echo from an abandoned past, uttering great words from which the original meanings have leaked away.

Nevertheless, the same listener who as "receiver" has decoding problems when he is presented with a religious message coded in the language and forms of thought of ancient times, is a man who as "destination" lives with the perennial hopes and fears of man in any age. If there ever was an age of faith, the sermon might serve some sort of simple reminder function, nudging the accepted tenets of the faith to the surface now and then to make them readily available for application. If our age is half as faithless as we are told, new and exciting possibilities open up for preaching as that one regular action by which a nonmetaphysical age might be helped to develop the metaphysics it so badly needs. Some preachers scold because their listeners are so badly educated in the faith that they can't properly hear the sermon. The complaint is oddly unprofessional. As a leader of a religious community, the preacher ought to find in the listener's problem a stimulus to deal with a fascinating problem in religious pathology, the problem of how to enable an instinctively religious animal to do something it greatly needs to do but which for the moment it cannot manage. *The opportunity of the preacher, then, is to make the sermon that act of religious communication which enables the listener to begin to make religious sense of his universe.* His task is not simply to deliver a message; it is to make it possible for the receiver to deal with messages of that sort. He has been taught that he must "preach the gospel." Actually, realistically, he must use the sermon as an occasion for helping people think about such things as gospels.

And now, with the aid of another simple model, let us begin to see how this might be done.

# 4

# From Data to Symbol: Models of Universes

To help people think about such things as gospels, the preacher must not only know something about gospels, but about *thinking,* and he must know more than what he has picked up by introspection during those occasions when he does a little thinking himself. For one function of the gospel is that of making sense of the universe. Let us add at once that the gospel is more than that; whenever someone seems to suggest that the gospel is a body of knowledge, such as a philosophy or a book of rules, we all feel a deep uneasiness, knowing what a travesty of gospel such a simple cognitive definition produces. But one function of gospel, we repeat without apology, is that of sense-making. The believer is a person who sees how all things work together for good. To be saved is to be saved at least from an ignorant, anguished confusion about what life is all about. For we are sense-making animals, creatures with "reason," and theologians can be forgiven a natural hyperbole when they try to describe God as the Supreme *Mind,* and ourselves as created in that image.

In any case, at the time of the sermon, whatever there is that is validly cognitive in Christianity becomes salient. Sermons have many purposes and travel on many communicative lines, but surely they should at least occasionally make sense and try from time to time to help people unravel some of the snarls that complicate the process of living. For we take seriously this sense-making function that is more than just a final, mature flowering of man's life, permitted to him when he has sufficient leisure. Our concern for the pastoral function of preaching, as an action designed to enable people to do better sense-making, is a concern rooted in a theory of man. And the best way to get at this is to locate sense-making biologically, in the very structure of the human animal, where it plays a unique part in both his evolution as a species and in his development as an individual. To exaggerate only a little, we take the preaching and hearing of sermons, and the kind of thinking that goes on when preaching occurs, to be a biological necessity for mankind. It constitutes the extreme case, which it exhibits in magnified form, of man's most typical behavior: forming models of his universe.

"Biological." We use the word deliberately. We take man to be an organism within an environment, and we consider his survival to depend on his capacity to learn about that environment by making sense of it.

Let us get at this fundamental matter by way of a parable.

*The Scientific American*, in an issue containing articles on the biosphere, that thin surface area on our planetary globe that supports life, published a picture of a fossil cell.[1] Seen through the microscope it is beautiful in its simplicity: the familiar circular form (in its two-dimensional representation) marking off the living organism from its surrounding environment. But what catches the philosophical imagination as we observe this is the date: *the cell is two billion years old.*

Such a picture gives a glimpse into a mystery, the long progression through the years of the emerging forms of living things in their unlikely battle against entropy. It suggests a certain toughness in the basic design of the living organism, a durability that argues a rightness in the pattern that for at least two billion years has maintained itself, changed and developed, and finally produced a descendent capable of contemplating its own past. For the cell exists by functioning as an input-output system, maintaining itself over against its environment as a separate entity organized for its own survival, yet only existing by virtue of its symbiotic relationship with that environment, so that we observe not just a picture of a cell, but of two things: cell, plus its essential world.

A film on the life of the cell, seen some two billion years later, might have this scenario of the parable in action.[2] We see the cell, looking remarkably like its ancient ancestor (but more complex, now possessing a nucleus). It absorbs nourishment through its wall, and ejects waste products, and it keeps these functions in delicate balance, existing over against its environment yet dependent upon it. Then, with surprising dramatic effect, the film illustrates the effect of dropping into the environmental bath some material hostile to the life of the cell. The cell shrinks; the input-output system is abruptly closed. We watch with concern this microcosmic moment of danger until the hostile material diffuses and the cell can return to normal, taking in nourishment, discarding waste. But then a more threatening substance is introduced into the environment. The cell acts defensively; it shrinks, hardening its skin, but to no avail. And as the camera records the scene through the microscope, a tragedy is enacted. The cell, attacked by substances too corrosive to resist, begins to disintegrate. Sections of the cell wall dissolve and drift away. The nutrient bath penetrates the cell's space. Before our eyes a complex world that has maintained its existence as a unity, a self, slides back irrevocably to disorder. One observes this minute disaster with an oddly acute sense of loss, as if the tragedy of all death is represented here in paradigm. The raw essence of even our own human existence seems to be demonstrated as only a special case of the basic condition of life: to learn the art of keeping two opposite functions in balance—to close the self against the world, lest the hard-won identity of the complex self be lost, and to open the self to the environment, lest the sustaining relationship to the nourishing nutrient bath be cut off.

Let us now move forward some billion years, to the time when life appears not only as simple cell but as that aggregate of cells we call human.

We draw from the parable of the cell at least this much wisdom: that the living organism lives by "knowing" in some way its environment. For cell or man, the original sin is *seclusion*. For man, the process of knowing is vastly more complex, but the initial proposition is maintained, magnified a thousandfold. The relationship of the human organism to its environment is also biological, as it is for our cellular ancestor, but for us there has developed an organ precisely adapted to implementing the relationship: the mind. With its network of receptors, its capacity to store and organize information and to exchange information with other minds, the mind assembles a vast amount of data about its world. The cell seems to us to operate with a certain mechanical simplicity, however elegant it may be in the efficiency of its responses. For us, an information processing system of great complexity and flexibility intervenes between stimulus and response, between the reception of information from the environment and action within it. And the essential part of that process of interest to us is the mind's ability to generate *symbols*.

To sketch a map of this formidable process and to identify some of the events that occur within it, we shall make use of a simple diagram. The diagram was never intended to bear the weight that we shall lay upon it, and it is so absurdly inadequate that it is safe to use, for we may not be tempted as we might by a better model to think of it as a picture of reality. It will be schematic, designed to focus our attention on essential elements of human information processing, and it will look very much like a microtome slice of that process, stained and mounted on a slide for our inspection.

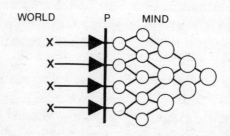

This "Margenau" diagram presents one of the simplest of devices—a line, drawn to separate the two realms, environment and organism, "world" and "mind." [3] The line, however, does not simply designate the separation of the two realities—the world out there, and my conscious self, thinking about it. It represents in schematic form the entire sensory equipment by which I receive data from the world. Margenau calls it the P-plane, to indicate that world and mind are linked as well as separated by my *perceptual* apparatus in all its complexity.

A digression: it may seem to those who remember their introductory course in philosophy that we have fallen into that old epistemological trap, the Cartesian dualism of *res extensa* and *res cogitans*. We shall, if all goes well, be rescued from it by precisely that element in the design that seems to have caused the trouble. For the P-plane, the perceptual process, does not so much separate as *join*. Mind and world are linked through it by a reciprocal activity. It does not mark the conjunction of two different kinds of reality, as it might in the Cartesian dualism. A biological view of mind reminds us that mind, and the entire human organism, was born within the world, and does not live within it as an alien being, a visitor from a different universe. Mind's capacity to know its world is a product of the world's function in shaping mind. When we come to consider the developmental history of mind, we shall abandon this static Margenau model for one that is more functional.

Like the Shannon model, the Margenau model is easily read. Events in the outer world impinge on the perceptual apparatus and generate responses that move from sense organ to brain. Diagrammed as closed circles, they suggest that they are a part of the perceptual system, a system open to observation and measurement. It is a system that seems to be a small universe, in which those astonishing organs—eye and ear—perform with a delicacy of response that has awakened devout admiration for centuries.

The perceptual system is then indicated as impinging upon the system of ideas, concepts, thoughts—which is in itself a universe—forming the third of those identified by the diagram: world, sensory system, and now, finally, the conceptual system. Because of our experience of the phenomenon "consciousness," we instinctively separate the conceptual world from its perceptual sources, but the mind-body problem continues to haunt us, and we know that we assert the detachment of mind from body in the face of evidence that seems at times to merge them. For the purposes of this essay we shall be rather frankly on the cognitive side, exploring the activity of mind as if it were capable, at least, of "freedom," and letting bodily and other controls on mind be discovered as necessary, if disconcerting, modifications of our cognitive bias.

As the diagram indicates, the conceptual system can be given at least a first description as "notions linked with other notions." Concepts seem to have some sort of individuality, and yet they seem also to exist only as parts of a system. And one of the linkages of great importance demands of the diagram an addition for which it is not exactly adapted—the rather awkward indication of the contribution of a cultural input to the conceptual system. It arrives, of course, by way of the sensory system; it is heard, and eventually read, as language, through formal and informal education, but it is also taken in through all the sights and sounds and smells which come from the exposure each person has because he lives in a certain time and place. All this is conceptualized, however, by the direct assistance of concepts fed to the growing mind from the fund available in the culture, of which language itself is a major part.

There is another input into the conceptual system which also strains the design of the model. The conceptual system receives inputs not only from the sensory system, as perceptual data picked up from the environment; it also receives emotional inputs, as if from the depths of the person. The conceptual life, insofar as it can be considered cognitive, seems to be a conceptualization of an inner environment as well as of an outer one. As with the mind-body problem, we can only file for future consideration this equally troublesome duality of idea and emotion.

The diagram then goes on to present its final statement (which is just as well since its usefulness is beginning to wear thin). Within the conceptual life, ideas seem to be identifiable in a hierarchy. Some ideas "organize" other ideas, as in the levels of abstraction among categories, in which *furniture* is more inclusive a concept than *chair*. But something like *a strain toward ultimates* is at work in the mind, a desire to formulate concepts that have greater and greater inclusiveness. That is, if a person starts the thinking process at all, chances are that sooner or later he shows tendencies of becoming a philosopher, and of having a theory about the totality of things. He constructs with increasing scope *a model of reality.*

Considered as a preliminary map of the area of our concern, this Margenau diagram has some obvious family resemblances to the Shannon diagram of the communication process. The process of thinking is a communication process in which the world is constantly sending to the mind a series of to-whom-it-may-concern messages. The reception of these by the mind moves from the immediate identification of stimuli to the construction of hypotheses about the stimulus and its context. Egon Brunswik has enlarged the Margenau diagram by dividing both sides of the P-plane into subsections. The diagram below is a schematic arrangement of Brunswik's ideas, which provide a visual parallel to the Margenau diagram.[4]

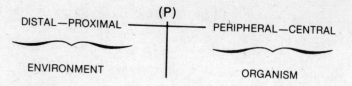

DISTAL—PROXIMAL ——— (P) ——— PERIPHERAL—CENTRAL

ENVIRONMENT | ORGANISM

The "proximal/peripheral" interface is the *perceptual* process where world and mind meet. The "central" area of the organism is the *conceptual* activity of mind, and it is the work of *cognition* to establish a successful match between "central" and "distal": a successful mapping in the central area of mind of the distal area of world. There is, of course, a continuing series of such mapping procedures as the mind checks hypotheses by selectively directing the perceptual process toward significant areas.

The essential issue that this Margenau diagram tries to reduce to graphic expression is the *detachment* of the cognitive life from the inputs that produce it. It spread out a spatial representation of the paradox of that life, which is a life born in and nourished by the perceptual experience of the body, and yet is also a life that seems to support the Cartesian positing of a different kind of reality from body. Reflection on this is probably as old as philosophy itself, going back at least to the time when philosophy became self-conscious, and began to ask how thinking was possible. As the classic philosophical question puts it, what is the nature and status of "ideas"? For ordinary experience presents us with the odd way that "general ideas," such as "horse," function. They have some sort of relationship with experiences of actual horses, and yet they "disregard the particulars in order to extract what is common," which is the Aristotelian notion. The "general" term "abstracts," as we say, from the particulars.[5] But how much life of its own does such an "abstraction" have? Reflection on this produced the long debates that reached a standoff in the nominalism-realism confrontation, and continued on into modern philosophical discussions until psychology freed itself as an academic discipline from the philosophy department and turned to research in concept formation.[6] Then it could tie concepts more closely to perceptual experience by working with such definitions of concepts as "common response to dissimilar stimuli." An important part of such research has been contributed by studies of language acquisition.

A major concern about the status of concepts is generated by an anxiety common to ordinary people and not only to philosophers, an anxiety about whether or not my ideas "correspond" to reality. Insofar as all thinking is detached from the environment, does it formulate for me a "true" model of reality? When psychology examines with care and precision the process of concept formation, even the philosopher hopes that the great question, the question of *Can I know the truth?* may be illuminated. We rather hope that in the long evolution of mind, something like a controlled, automatic response that links *world event, perceptual response,* and *idea,* will have given to the end product, *idea,* an inevitable rightness that guarantees that our thinking is, indeed, true thinking about the world out there. We hope that a detailed exposition of this process in its simpler forms may make more complicated forms of reflection seem equally valid.

Yet we know that the hope is futile. Automated responses are indeed made by minds, as we shall see, but with the emergence of *mind,* the processing of information became capable of a fantastic degree of flexibility, and therefore at the cost of an uncertainty that is never to be removed. We learn about the world through a process that

43

never is completed, making and testing hypotheses, revising them, knowing when to abandon the hunch that had seemed at first to promise so much but which has served its purposes and must go—all the delicate apparatus of the learning process becomes man's opportunity and his fate.

For most ordinary purposes, this information processing system works very well. We do, after all, survive, and survive by the successful learning we do, discovering what is dangerous out there and what is benevolent. And no man has to go it alone; the process is social. Cultural memories and accumulated experience replace in man the genetic programming, physically inherited, that in other species governs their responses to the stimuli from the environment. We accumulate over the centuries a system of coded findings, ranging all the way from the elements of language to large scale statements about the universe, and by various forms of education this is carefully transmitted to each new generation.

But as we contemplate those "larger" concepts that in the Margenau diagram are farthest away from the P-plane, it seems evident that all these questions of certainty and uncertainty, of survival value, of arbitrariness, of cultural inheritance, must now be applied with a difference. Paradoxes emerge. Talk about ultimates may be the hardest to test and verify, yet we may hold ultimate ideas with the greatest resistance to change, as if they were the most certain. Ultimates may seem detached from the immediate realities, yet they may seem to deal with matters of survival. Differences among cultures about ultimates may seem to suggest that such ideas are "arbitrary" constructs of the imagination, yet we often claim as we move away from the P-plane into the farther reaches of the cognitive realm that we encounter new and strange behaviors in the life of the concepts that operate there.

The Margenau diagram will have done enough if it stimulates this sort of extended meditation on these familiar aspects of the cognitive process. For thinking is at once the most familiar thing in the universe and the oddest. We do it all the time, yet, if we stop to think about thinking, it becomes so strange an activity that one wonders how anyone does it at all. And while the mystery extends even to the simplest kinds of cognitive response to stimuli, even, that is, to baby's first word, yet it seems to be true that as one moves toward the right of the Margenau diagram, one moves into realms of thinking of greater and greater difficulty. Some kinds of thinking are more detached, more uncertain, more arbitrary, less communicable, than others. But these are just the kinds of thinking that are demanded of us in the preaching and hearing of sermons.

It would seem to be necessary for anyone who attempts to "improve" the contents of a mind, such as a teacher or preacher, or indeed anyone interested in changing the ideas in a mind, that he understand how ideas are formed. For the preacher especially, our theme will be that the sermon must be designed not only to be an expression of some needed and useful truth, but designed so that it enables the listener to do the kind of thinking that the reception of such truths requires. The preacher must become a physician of minds, alert to the very pathologies of thought that his subject matter induces, for he is asking his listener to do just that kind of cognitive work that most of us come to rather awkwardly.

Given this overview of the area, then, let us turn to an examination of a miracle: the way that the human organism develops the cognitive equipment which the right side of the Margenau diagram maps with absurdly simple lines and circles. It is a development that moves through an astounding range. W. C. Fields, defeated all his life by dogs and children and therefore hating them with a rich, frightened malevolence, once had to make a movie with a small child, the famous Baby LeRoy. As the infant was carried onto the set, Fields looked at the little scene-stealer with deep distrust and said, "Your line is *goo-goo*. Don't muff it." What other living organism moves, in its developing life, from the level of goo-goo to that of the poets? (The miracle has been described more elegantly by the title of a book on Christian education, *From Cry to Word*.)[7] As we make an attempt to summarize some of the things known about this miraculous transformation, remember that we engage in this to learn as much as we can about man's ability to make any cognitive sense about his world so that we may design strategies for helping him make ultimate sense of his universe. Be prepared to find the enterprise both fascinating and difficult, and to end with only bits and pieces of understanding, very much less than any adequate strategy needs.

# 5

# How to Carve Up a Universe: Perception

To make sense of a world one must observe it, and not as an undifferentiated blur but as a collection of entities that are identifiable, and that take their place in relationships that can be plotted and organized. But the basic action is "seeing"; we are sighted animals, able to stand at a distance from the universe and be "objective," getting it into "perspective." The language of visual perception is the language of philosophy.

So we make sense of the world perceptually. We make "sense"—the word is more accurate than we usually notice. The detachment that the cognitive process achieves begins in the attachments of body to world through the perceptual equipment.

From merely sensate life to fully cognitive life has been an evolution long in development. It would help us to understand that progression if we could observe its history on the planet over three billion years. Does each infant recapitulate that history? Perhaps he does, but in any case his cognitive growth seems to give us a slow-motion instant replay of the process, and helps us to separate out some of the elements for a less confusing view than the mature mind of an adult presents. There is another advantage to the developmental approach, and to state it is to formulate a thesis which our examination of the perceptual contributions to cognition is designed to demonstrate: cognition originates in perception, and perception both nourishes and inhibits cognitive growth. Perception, as the protomental activity in which cognition is born, continues to exert a gravitational attraction on the efforts of cognition to achieve escape velocity. The making of concepts is a difficult art, and while the human organism seems driven by its very nature to do it, nevertheless, as we shall see, it has a tendency to slip back, to evade the often hard work of conceptualizing and to substitute for it simpler ways of processing environmental data.

The first years of the life of the mind present us with what will be the persistent drama of that life: the conflict, or at least the tension, between the inputs of data to the mind from the environment and the models by which the mind organizes that data. We remind ourselves of the occupational hazard of all philosophical thinking: every model of the universe is both an aid to understanding the world, and a screen that filters out data that does not support the model. It is the intention of these present explorations into the beginnings and early history of conceptualizing to show how deeply this hazard is built in to the normal and daily processes of thinking. Man is a philosopher in spite of himself, because he cannot help but philosophize, but the processing equipment that he must use, even in its simpler, apparently safer forms, is a source of error as well as of truth.

For a guide to the early development of this process, we follow the work of Jean Piaget.[1] From Piaget we learn to view the mind as a sensitive organism growing within its environment, and to see it as developing capacities according to a schedule of growth.

Piaget speaks of thinking as the happy combination of two processes. "Assimilation" is the reading by the mind of reality as it is encountered, assimilating it to whatever categories the mind may have available. It is matched by "accommodation" in which the categories are themselves changed to provide more workable responses. We assimilate the world to our models; we accommodate our models to the world. The process continues through changing stages of equilibrium.

From birth, then, the child who seems so separate, so enclosed within its own skin, is like the primitive cell, an organism within an environment. The cell in its nutrient bath has a relatively fixed system of responses to its environment, with a programmed set of interchanges with it that establishes the limits for its survival. The human infant has greatly expanded capacities for this process, and Piaget follows and describes their stages of development.

The first stage, from birth to about age eighteen months, Piaget terms the "sensori-motor" period, before the infant has acquired language. It is a time of remarkable mental development, "for it is during this time that the child constructs all the cognitive substructures that will serve as a point of departure for his later perceptive and intellectual development."[2] He constructs "a complex system of action-schemes" and learns to organize reality "in terms of spatio-temporal and causal structures."[3] Piaget takes us through six substages of the growth of the child as he forms in what we might call a preabstract way an understanding of his world. At first, Piaget says, "the child's initial universe is entirely centered on his own body and action in an egocentrism as total as it is unconscious. . . ." He continues:

> In the course of the first eighteen months, however, there occurs a kind of Copernican revolution, or, more simply, a kind of general decentering process whereby the child eventually comes to regard himself as an object among others in a universe that is made up of permanent objects (that is, structured in a spatio-temporal manner) and in which there is at work a causality that is both localized in space and objectified in things.[4]

A universe of permanent objects. At first, an object that has been observed by an infant and then hidden from him no longer exists. Then comes an important transition, when the child begins to search for the hidden object, and recognizes it when it reappears. From this the child learns to play his first metaphysical game: *peek-a-boo,* discovering with delight that the universe exists out there even when it is not perceived. One wishes for the chance to overhear a conversation on this matter between Piaget and Bishop Berkeley!

It would be difficult to find two philosophical issues of greater importance than the questions of the status of "permanent objects," and of the effects of seeing the world from the self as center. As to the first, "the scheme of the permanent object is closely related to the whole spatio-temporal and causal organization of the practical universe."[5] The child's interactions with his universe pass through stages that culminate in a recognition of a world operating in independence of him, and with his increasing awareness of the special behavior of certain objects to be identified as other persons, he discovers other centers of causality than himself. He is engaged in what Piaget calls "the construction of Reality," [6] and Piaget stresses the importance of the child's *actions* in this work. The child's sensori-motor actions operate like a series of basic scientific experiments directed toward the discovery of the properties of the external world.

These "cognitive substructures," which represent the first steps of man as philosopher, receive a major modification at the end of the sensori-motor period by the emergence of what Piaget calls "the semiotic or symbolic function." It consists in the ability to represent something (a signified something: object, event, conceptual scheme, etc.) by means of a "signifier" which is differentiated and which serves only a representative purpose: language, mental image, symbolic gesture, and so on.[7] Of these, language may be the most important. Lenneberg and others consider language to be a species-specific trait, making its appearance when the organism has matured physically, "appearing at a certain time in the child's physical development and following a fixed sequence of events." [8] The importance of the acquisition of language cannot be stressed too much; if there are, indeed, nonlinguistic forms of thought, it is nevertheless language that becomes the vehicle for the further development of intelligence, and our understanding of the growth and use of concepts will have language as one of its essential parameters.

With language, and the semiotic function in general, the child advances rapidly in his long and elaborate process of forming conceptual models of his universe. Here Piaget sets before us one of his most illuminating glimpses into intellectual development. During the period between ages two and eleven (these ages are approximate) the child is working with concepts, using a language and receiving instruction in the accumulated wisdom of his culture as an addition to his own efforts to conceptualize his experience. Yet for the first part of this period, his conceptional life shows certain hindrances. The learnings of his sensori-motor period are only translated with some difficulty into conceptual form. The concepts now available to him from the public domain presuppose a more complete freeing of himself from the egocentrism that dominated his earlier years than he can manage. In short, he makes missteps on the way toward the art of abstracting.

The famous experiments related to "conservation" show whether or not the child has made the transition to such thinking (to the level of what Piaget calls "concrete operations").[9] The contents of a glass are poured into a narrower glass, resulting in a higher water level. The question is then put, do we now have more water in the second glass, or not? Until about the age seven, a child will say that there is now more liquid in the taller glass. His judgment is based on the perceptual evidence of the water levels; he is not yet able to use so abstract a notion as *volume, for which shape is irrelevant.* Two lines, one straight, the other wavy, are taken to be of the same length when they are drawn one below the other, with the ends matching; each line appears to go the same distance so they are of equal "length." A ball of clay is said to have less clay in it than the same clay rolled out in the shape of a sausage. In a variety of similar experiments, the child's understanding of the situation seems to be misled by perceptual cues. When the child is old enough, he is able to achieve "conservation" (that is, to "conserve" certain properties such as volume in spite of changes in appearances) and he then does just what you and I do. He says, "Of course there is just as much water as before. It's just that the water level is higher in the narrow container." The idea of volume without consideration of shape is an idea of too great abstraction for the child before the ages of seven or eight. The perceptual cues mislead, but also the very action of pouring, in the experiment involving water levels, is taken as having "results that are literally incalculable." Afterward, the changes can be observed as events "decentered from the action of the subject," [10] and therefore reversible, transformations taking place in an independent and external world.

This transition represents the development of philosophical powers from "appearances" to "realities," to use terms once fashionable in philosophical circles. The child is demonstrating the importance of one of the most ancient of philosophical arts, to discern the structures that lie beneath the surface of things. For Piaget, a certain cognitive maturing is necessary for this, as if the child recapitulated in his growing years some ideal progress of philosophy itself from being captured by the way things *seem* to actually knowing the way things *are*. His growth is in "intelligence," the capacity to construct more adequate conceptual models.

The last stage of cognitive development, from eleven to fifteen, is the period of "formal" operations, "a transformation of thought that permits the handling of hypotheses and reasoning with regard to propositions removed from concrete and present observation." [11] In this third stage, "the subject becomes capable of reasoning correctly about propositions he does not believe, or at least not yet; that is, propositions that he considers pure hypotheses." [12] Moving further to the right of the Margenau diagram, he becomes capable of working with propositions, free from the manipulation of possible cases and actual observations.

We have selected from the extensive work of Piaget these impressionistic sketches of one of his main themes to focus our attention on one aspect of the mind's development: its emergence from its perceptual, sensory beginnings. This is the major theme of that development, and Piaget reveals it to be a progressive freeing of the cognitive life from the distortions of its perceptual origins. It is as if the history of the developing mind recapitulates the history of science, becoming increasingly more adept at the task of framing conceptual models of the reality encountered perceptually in the world.

Philosophical reflection on the perceptual process and its contribution to knowledge is as old as philosophy itself.[13] Are there innate ideas, or is there nothing in the intellect that has not come by way of the senses? The argument goes round and round, and we do not propose to join the dance. But we cannot evade at least a minimal examination of the perceptual process, for the act of communicating raises questions about sensory awareness, and the act of philosophical and religious communication puts to the listener a perceptual question, among others, by asking, "What do you *see*, and what do you make of it?" From Piaget we learn that the life of the mind begins in sensory processes, but also that as the mind develops, sensory processes continue to operate in the knowing that becomes increasingly cognitive. For the religious communicator, and especially for the preacher who has not much time and who must often work without the benefit of feedback, nothing is more important than knowing how free the minds are that he addresses. How free, that is, from automatic responses, or

54

from the captivating power of certain images, or from the misleading evidence of visual data. He is concerned to know how well his listeners can handle the ancient philosophical problem of making sense of what is observed, and of separating appearance and reality. He must become adept at diagnosing the powerful effects of perception on the reflective life of the mind. As one who deals with believing, he must know about seeing.

We shall be working with the hypothesis that the perceptual process exerts a powerful governing power over the philosophical development of most of us. The first philosophical insights may come through our first muscular actions in what Piaget calls the sensori-motor stage, but it is the perceptual life, in which visual perception seems to be especially important, that teaches us our first philosophical lessons. It is tempting to make a premature and sweeping generalization, and to say that it is the power of perceptual experience that shapes in us steadily and relentlessly over the years, *an "instinctive" naive metaphysics,* unexamined because it is so natural as to be unnoticed, and yet in conflict with the metaphysic which is presupposed by such a religion as Christianity. To continue the hypothesis: the receiving of a communication about Christianity might well be hindered or distorted by the conflict between these two metaphysics. Indeed, such a conflict may be the psychological dimension of what contemporary Christians experience as a "crisis of faith." We have traced that crisis often back to sociological origins in science and technology, but science, which has extended with intensity and precision the perceptual process, may be considered to have given cultural reinforcement to what is basically a natural psychological influence. Perhaps every man, simply because he is human, and because his reflection about the world must be done by a mind dependent upon the development of perceptual and cognitive processes, develops naturally certain philosophical positions which might be thought of as the product of his psychological structure.

Even a brief glance into any general review of the perceptual process reveals it to be an extraordinary project in receiving, interpreting, categorizing, and in various other ways processing the vast amounts of data which the perceptual system feeds into the mind.[14] Strategies for handling it simply have to be developed. Nonhuman forms of life can respond more directly to perceptual inputs.

Consider this diagrammatic figure:

Cut out of stiff cardboard, it is passed like a shadow over ducks or geese. Moving from left to right, it is ignored; the shadow is that of a *goose*. Moving from right to left it throws the fowl into a state of panic; the shadow is that of a *hawk*. This is genetically programmed behavior, not a behavior that is learned. For the fowl, simple perception must be that intelligent for survival.

Decision-making for the survival of man, however, has been moved more and more into the realm of active consciousness, and perceptual data must be checked against stored information. Born with no automatic responses, we must identify hostile aircraft by learning their profiles.

But what we have gained in flexibility has been at a price. We are surrounded by stimuli, and would go mad if we had to think about all of them. For sheer sanity's sake we must learn the arts of selection, delegating what we can to automatic procedures, like good executives.

At one extreme, as the experiments in sensory deprivation demonstrate, a certain level of stimuli seems essential for sanity. The McGill University volunteers who were placed in situations of minimum sensory stimuli experienced deep anxiety, and such perceptual aberrations as hallucinations.[15] But for ordinary experience, the problem is overload. Brown and Lenneberg have determined that the eye can discern 7,500,000 separable hues, but our linguistic processing of this amazing range of inputs indicates the degree to which we reduce this to manageable limits. English has about 4,000 words to deal with color, of which eight are in common use.[16] We have, to use an engineering term commonly borrowed to discuss this psychological matter, a fairly narrow perceptual channel. In a classic article, "The Magical Number Seven, Plus or Minus Two," Miller replicated an experiment performed in the late nineteenth century by Jevons.[17] If a handful of marbles is tossed on the floor, and we are permitted only a quick glimpse of them, we can remember their position with some accuracy if the number is small. We reach our peak at what Miller called "the magical number seven, plus or minus two." Poor observers, or poor rememberers, may become inaccurate at five; good ones can go on to nine. It is seven for most of us.

The need for controlling our sensory inputs can also be

demonstrated by what has been called the "cocktail effect." [18] In a room full of people at a party, a bedlam of sound assaults our ears, but by selective attention we can attend to the conversation of the one or two people with whom we are discussing a matter of interest. The rejected sound is entering our perceptual systems, however, and the fact can be demonstrated by experiment. Moray has shown that when two different sound tracks are fed into two earphones, and we are directed to attend to only one of them, we will notice at once if our own name is secretly inserted in the rejected track as a part of the message.[19] It is as if all messages are heard, but we have been forced of necessity to develop ways of selecting and discarding.

Similar channel limitations are imposed by the operation of the memory system.[20] Short-term memory, for example, rapidly discards inputs that need not be retained; were this not so, reading would be difficult, or perhaps impossible. The visual images of the words just read would pile up in a confusing jumble. Short-term memory files them away for a short time for recall as necessary, but to go on to the next group of words, we must process what we have just perceived. Even in the initial perceptual encounter we bunch together a selected group of words. The whole process seems to be one of funneling, the successive reduction of large quantities of data to make it manageable.

The channeling and controlling of perceptual inputs can result in remarkable efficiency of operation for relatively simple organisms. For a man, a somewhat complicated organism, but nevertheless largely dependent on his perceptual equipment for knowledge of his world, it is important to know how much he has inherited of the perceptual behaviors which have dominated organic life throughout his evolutionary history. Since the content, shape, and quality of our total response to our world is the stuff of which our philosophies are formed, it is important to us to know the operation of our built-in selectors, the strategies by which we make *automatic* our decisions to see, remember, and eventually bring under sense-making judgment the data that bombards us.

At the level of simple perception it is instructive to discover how much decision-making is done by the perceptual equipment in simply seeing.[21] Two fascinating recent books can open this world to the reader, and their titles express their themes: *The Intelligent Eye*, by R. L. Gregory, and *Visual Thinking*, by Rudolph Arnheim.[22] Very early in life, the infant must "learn" that the curved image received on the retina, coded and transferred to the cerebral cortex, and constantly changing (as when he sees a glass of water being moved about) is nevertheless the visual report of an unchanging object. Even now, as we look at the oval top of the glass, we "know" it to be circular. We move our heads, and the room remains "steady." But if we move an eye with a finger, the room jumps; we have by-passed some of the adjustment processes which usually impose stability on the observed scene.

This discussion of the "constancies" follows the logic of most discussions of perceptual process by deliberately blurring the distinction between what happens at the sensory organ and what happens somewhere in the brain. When Arnheim writes chapters entitled "The Intelligence of Perception," he is stretching the application of both words. "Perception" becomes an action involving sensory organs and also the transmission and reception of the information generated within them. Arnheim says concerning the perception of shape:

In the perception of shape lie the beginnings of concept formation. Whereas the optical image projected upon the retina is a mechanically complete recording of its physical counterpart, the corresponding visual percept is not. The perception of shape is the grasping of structural features found in, or imposed upon, the stimulus material. . . . Perception consists in fitting the stimulus material with templates of relatively simple shape, which I call visual concepts or visual categories.[23]

Our seeing of a three-dimensional universe is done by the automatic translation of visual data into cognitive conclusions about the world out there, and we exaggerate only slightly when we think of this as an important bit of philosophizing done within the unnoticed workings of the perceptual system.

Certain perceptual experiences can overtax this system and throw it into error or confusion, bringing it suddenly to our attention. Visual illusions present data that is just ambiguous enough to trick the automatic visual process.[24] The Necker cube, for example, offers the visual system a complex of lines that can be read in two ways, and either hypothesis is "reasonable." [25]

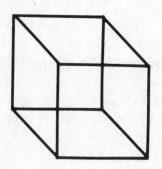

The eye sees the cube as from below, or from above, and alternates between the two equally possible interpretations. Automatic visual processing has done its best with the situation and consciousness must step in to work on the problem of deciding just what is out there. Optical illusions remind us of the arbitrary element in our ordinary acts of seeing, which for most purposes work with great efficiency, converting a two-dimensional image into a "perception" (part sensory, part cognitive) of a three-dimensional world so that we find our way around in it with ease. The chapter on perception in any good textbook on psychology opens up for us the astonishing skill that the visual system develops, such as its ability to "recognize" when given only a few visual clues. It is evident that when we "see what is there," the perceptual process receives visual data that is coded by the retina and must be decoded before what we call "seeing" can occur. The whole process proceeds as much as possible below the level of conscious attention. It takes the odd case, such as the experience of receiving sight as an adult after years of blindness, to reveal how much there is of learned interpretation in the act of seeing.[26] The familiar trapezoid window illusion of Adelbert Ames demonstrates the power of the cognitive associations that experience has tied to certain visual inputs.[27] The trapezoid window rotates slowly, but the eye sees it as *oscillating*. Unlike some visual illusion, however, the eye continues to see the window oscillate even after the observer knows that the window is rotating in a complete circle. The visual clues he is receiving are locked in, so to speak, to a particular cognitive reading, and one's conscious effort to see what one knows to be there is defeated by the power of the perceptual habit that "reads" the narrower edge of the window as "distant."

If we depend on our perceptual equipment to do as

much automatic perceptual processing as possible, and if this processing is educated in its work by a long history of fairly successful matchings of perceptions and cognitive conclusions concerning our world, is it possible that this strategy may educate us at a deeper level? It has been suggested that the city dweller lives in what has been called a "fabricated universe," [28] a world of straight lines, parallels, right angles, and similar geometrical regularities. Evidently, our long experience with such visual conditions can provide the conditions that make certain visual illusions "work." There is some evidence that the Ames trapezoid window illusion, which depends upon our long experience with the perspective effects of rectangular objects, is less effective as an illusion when observed by people who do not live in a world of rectangles.[29] Perhaps that experience also forms in us philosophical expectations; our visual experience would be a medium with a message of its own. McLuhan's remarks about the effects of reading printed lines that present ideas in linear sequence would be a special case of the formative influence of more general visual experience.[30] Edward Carpenter contrasts our experience with that of the Eskimo:

> The familiar Western notion of enclosed space is foreign to the Eskimo. Both snow igloos and skin tents lack vertical walls and horizontal ceilings; no planes parallel each other and none intersects at ninety degrees. There are no straight lines, at least none of any length. Rectangles are unknown. Euclidean space is a concept unique to literate man.[31]

And Carpenter describes Eskimo art as being the expression of this experience:

62

A distinctive mark of Eskimo art is that many of the ivory carvings, generally of sea animals, will not stand up, but roll clumsily about. Each lacks a single, favored point of view and hence a base. They were never intended to be set in place and viewed, but rather to be worn and handled, turned this way and that. I knew a trader with a fine, showpiece collection of such carvings who solved this problem by lightly filing each piece "on the bottom" to make it stand up, but alas he also made them stationary, something the carver never intended.[32]

Carpenter went from Eskimo country to Russia, finding there an epitome of the linear response to a fabricated surrounding world: "Everything visual requires a single point of view—a review position, like Stalin reviewing troops; all painting is in three dimensional perspective; every plaza is to be viewed from X." [33]

It would be going too far with unsupported speculation to say that the ordinary visual (and other sensory) experiences in a culture determine that culture's instinctive metaphysics, tilting it toward an expectancy of regularity, logic, fixed structure, and the like. But the question persists, stimulated by cross-cultural studies, by the implications of the history of art forms, by our awareness of the importance of such basic visual and sensory experiences in forming ideas of the self, and by our awareness of how steeped we are in a "perspective" world, seen from a vantage point, constructed by ourselves to be secure and manageable.[34] It is a question to which we must continually return as we search for the shaping forces that make our imaginations what they are, and determine what kinds of thinking are possible for us.

To these remarks about the way that visual and other

forms of perception may shape our minds in hidden, preliminary ways, let us now add some comments on a process that seems to operate in the opposite direction. For the mind, taught by its sensory experience, and viewing its world under the tutelage of automated perceptual responses, tries hard to maintain that view by overriding any perceptual evidence that might contradict what it has learned. The mind sees what it expects, or what it wants to see, or what it finds familiar and therefore manageable. A classic experiment has been made concerning "binocular rivalry." [35] A device presented two pictures in brief exposures, one to each eye. One picture represented a bullfight scene, the other, a scene from a baseball game. Viewers came from two groups, Mexicans and American. When both pictures were presented simultaneously at tachistoscopic exposures, the Mexicans saw only the bullfight, and the Americans saw only the baseball game. Observed at very brief exposures, incomplete circles are seen as complete, nonsense groups of letters are seen as familiar words. And in more complex behaviors, taboo words are seen as ordinary words, and in this case, the ordinary words may have little visual similarity to the taboo words; the mind has imposed a more "proper" word, and that is what is "seen." [36]

We are describing, here, mental behavior that can range from simple occasions, in which the mind does (so to speak) what comes most easily, to behaviors that involve important conceptual judgments. When a cognitive process can override perceptual data, the way is paved for imposing on the universe a theory, an illicit descriptive notion, and what began as the mind's strategy for managing automatically the complexity of data that pours in on it thus ends as a strategy of misinterpretation.

Its power for doing this is very great. A series of experiments involving ambiguous stimuli is worth noting, for it is the ambiguous, incongruent, confusing data that often is the most important for anyone trying to "read" his universe. In such ambiguities lurk the corrective data that can produce essential modifications of theories, and how we handle what is not clear controls our capacity to learn.

One set of experiments begins by presenting to an observer a picture well out of focus, and then slowly bringing the image into clear focus as the observer watches.[37] For those who experience the experiment from the beginning, a common response is to decide early in the process the content of the picture. The vague mass of light and dark patches seems to trigger a decision process that anxiously searches for solution to the visual problem. Like Hamlet (feigning madness), it sees a camel or a whale in the cloud formations. Then, as the image is brought into sharper focus, this initial decision is usually not confirmed by the more precise visual data now available. But the observer begins, subconsciously, to find confirmation for his initial hypothesis, and in extreme cases, he may look at the now completely clear image, and continue to see what he had earlier assumed it to be. Not to be able to "see what is there" is an experience that produces anxiety. A survival skill is threatened, and we work hard at restoring it. Many of us have both been intrigued and distressed by the photograph of masses of light and shade which, we are told, is a face, or a dog; we try to see it, and discover that we are at the mercy of a visual process which only works, when it does, automatically. We hope for recognition to explode; the Gestalt cannot be put together by a simple addition of the obvious elements. In the experiment with the gradually clarifying image, it is interesting to note that observers who begin watching after the picture is partly in focus can revise their judgment more easily than those who experienced the full sequence. The conclusion derived from the experiment is that when a decision is made concerning ambiguous stimuli, a person has enough investment in the achievement so that he is prevented from making a change; those with less investment can revise their visual hypothesis more easily.

A special form of this experiment uses the device for presenting two different pictures, one to each eye.[38] The pictures are of two faces. As the experiment begins, one face only is lighted; the other is dark, and not visible. As the experiment proceeds, the light gradually dims from the first picture, and the light begins to illuminate the second. Observers are commonly unaware that they are now seeing a different face; they observe the second face, fully lighted, while the first is now dark and invisible, and see no change. When both faces are then lighted, they often exhibit great anxiety and confusion. It is a painful experience to find that you have been looking at one thing and seeing another.

A famous demonstration presents a film in which Mosjakhin, a Russian actor, is seen in three close-ups, one in conjunction with a view of a bowl of soup on a table, a second with a view of a dead woman in a coffin, and the third with a scene of a small girl and a funny toy.[39] The viewers of the film express astonishment at the range and versatility of the actor's response to these three quite different scenes. Yet the close-up of the actor's face used each time is the same; the changes in his expression were imposed on the face by the expectation of the viewer. One is reminded of the effect of "indexing": a picture of a couple at a railway station is seen as sad when entitled "The Parting," and as happy when entitled "The Arrival."

In all these experiments, the intention is to probe into the ways that our perceptual and cognitive strategies for handling overload of input, ambiguity, novelty, and the like, become hindrances to the necessary task of receiving and processing data impinging upon us from our environment. Perhaps no one ever was so naive as to think that to make sense of a universe, one simply needs to look it over carefully, note what is there, and organize conclusions about it. But when one reads of these and many other experiments that demonstrate the fallibility of even the simpler perceptual processes, and the many ways by which the strategies of the mind which evolved for its operation can turn against it without sounding any sort of warning, then the suspicion grows that the work of conclusion-making is dangerous business, open to more aberrations than we ordinarily suspect. The teachers who participated in the Rosenthal experiments could not believe, when it was over, that it could have happened.[40] In that experiment, teachers were told that their classes had either low or high IQ's, although each class was a normal mixture. At the end of the experiment, the teachers had, somehow, produced classes that did, in fact, test out to the IQ that the teacher assumed the children had. How they produced the effect is still a mystery. After five years of careful study of the films and tapes of the teacher-class behavior, the experimenters have been unable to observe the subtle cues by which the teacher induced the "appropriate" behaviors into the children. Producing ideas that we either expect, or handle best, can be a delicate, yet astonishingly tough, behavior.

This brief review of the perceptual process has identified two similar behaviors. The first of these is the capacity of the perceptual system to develop automatic responses, as when the eye reads the changing visual cues presented to it as we move about a room, and reports to the brain "business as usual," a square room with walls that do not move. Complex data is translated to present a model of the world, a model that presupposes consistency and regularity in the universe. The more this process can operate without demanding our conscious attention, the better it is for us, and the system operates with a high level of success. We might call this the Centipede Factor: if the centipede stops to wonder what foot moves next, he is lost. The other behavior has to do with the world on the basis of the data which we accept from our sensory processes. And while automatic sorts of responses are what might be called a virtue for immediate sensation, they can cause trouble for conscious behavior by becoming conclusions that prevent the reception of new data. We are familiar with the way that a large theory can control how a person sees life, but it is important to notice that the power of a theory to screen out corrective data can operate at the level of fairly elementary perception. We are, it is true, creatures with exceptionally sensitive sensory abilities, and clearly we must develop strategies for handling masses of perceptual data. The lesson seems to be that this is necessary at simple levels of perception, reasonably safe at medium levels, and dangerous at higher levels. Given a bombardment of data, the organism adopts a natural strategy, borrowed from simpler organisms: *make all responses as automatic as possible.* At the medium level, when we must decide, for example, what it is we are seeing, one might suppose that new perceptual data would be strong enough to override a faulty decision as to what it is that is out there to be seen. That is why the experiments dealing with ambiguity are so important. Because I have decided that I know what it is I am looking at, I can stare at contradictory data and not register the correction. Even at the level of raw perceptual input, I can "see" what I think is there. The paradox of the perceptual process is this: that as a way of living with its remarkable sensitivity which produces great quantities of data, the organism must impose premature or inaccurate closure upon its reception of data in order to manage it. There emerges from this a basic insight concerning method: to the degree that it is difficult to *construct* a model, it is difficult to *change* such a model. We give up our hard-earned understanding of our world with a quite natural reluctance. And since they have value, they deserve our respect, but since they are not perfect, they need revision. The adjustment of these contradictory demands is the essential skill that the philosopher must learn. And he works with a natural bias toward keeping any model he has made; as an organism, he has inherited a bias toward fixity, but he lives in a complex universe, and fixity of response is not an adequate method for processing all the data that impinges upon him from his environment.

Anyone who contemplates the mysterious process by which data from the environment become translated into the realm of symbols, to be accepted as "knowledge of the world," must hesitate with many unanswered questions before the phenomenon of perception. It seems to contain within itself the entire anatomy of philosophy, miniaturized. Within perception occurs the crucial event for knowing—the coding process by which one kind of reality (the environment) is translated into another kind of reality (symbolic knowledge).

We take perception to be not only a compendium of mysteries, but somehow basic, in the sense of being that part of the knowing process which comes first, and has some sort of determining function that controls what comes later. How a person *looks at the world,* taking that phrase in its literal sense, seems to give an important clue for understanding how he looks at it philosophically. How much of his perception does he *automate,* and how much of it does he *cognitively override?*

Such questions send us on to consider the cognitive process, separated out, for convenience, from its functioning within the perceptual-cognitive process of which it is a part.

# 6

# How to Carve Up
# a Universe: Cognition

"How a person looks at the world": that deceptively simple phrase defines for us the general area of our concern. Man is the animal who must look at his world with care—and understand it—if he is to survive. The bombardment of information received by his sensory equipment pours in upon a complex and sophisticated processing equipment, but man does more than just receive, passively, an input of data. Such passivity would be an appropriate part of an automatic response system. But the human animal short-circuits many of its inputs, putting them through a processing procedure that provides the means for checking them against stored information, and then acts with varying degrees of originality and freedom to search for more data.

It is that middle ground, where experience is matched with wisdom, that concerns us now.

When the preacher stands before a group of people, ready to preach to them on some subject, he devoutly hopes that he can interest them in *thinking about it.* He may also hope to move them emotionally, and possibly change their overt behavior, but preaching is very much a cognitive event for both preacher and listener. It is the time when everyone may pause to reflect on the meaning of some aspect of life. Sermons may slide away from reflections on meanings, but a major ingredient of preaching is cognitive.

The preacher, then, stands before a group of people in the expectation that what he does will get them thinking, and about rather difficult subjects, inviting them to do a kind of thinking that they seldom do. He is expected to do some of this for them; encouraging them to go along with him, and is given the special time and place to do it, being the authoritative person who is trained in the art. He is the person who can think about ultimates.

Thinking about ultimates is ordinary thinking carried, so to speak, to extremes. If there is a cognitive process which operates by some sort of divinely guided action of the mind, unknown to the uninitiated—such as inspired or ecstatic utterances—we shall not deal with that here. For our purposes, the cognitive work done by all concerned during the sermon is ordinary in its procedures, however odd its subject matter.

This means that the preacher must be concerned about how his listeners do any kind of thinking at all. The odd subject to which he will lead them will stretch their capacity for thought, and to help them with it he must see its kinship with all thinking. To put it in a word, he is concerned with their capacity for finding *meaning.*

The human organism exists by the construction of meanings. Unlike simpler forms of life, it develops the capacity for deciding ("consciously," as we label the mysterious process) what is going on out there and within himself. A person develops that inner life that seems to mirror reality, constructing in the mind the symbolic forms that represent a world. He moves from learning the names of objects to theoretical models that attempt to describe their behavior and on to creative designs for possible alternative universes. He probably could not do very much of this if he could not receive from others the accumulated findings of past thinkers. The making of meanings is a social behavior.

Into this enormous subject we can only go a little way, but into it we must go, for the preacher is a part of the system of social agencies that are concerned with meaning: education, the mass media, and the arts. It is not enough for him to be orthodox in content; he must understand something of how meanings are made by each of us and add to that some special knowledge of how to help us make ultimate meanings. For he is, in the best sense of the word, an educator.

Our concern will be with large meanings, with concepts, that is, of great inclusiveness: *love, forgiveness,* the "organizing concepts" that are designed to make sense of great portions of experience. And our approach to this can be stated at once: the shaping of such concepts is difficult and comes late in human development, and, therefore, we need all the help we can get when we try to deal with such ideas. Furthermore, to extend that to the sermon: every sermon must have, in addition to its message, the function of helping the listener to hear the message by enabling him to handle ideas of higher generality. The sermon must be both educational and therapeutic; it must raise ultimate questions and assist us to think about them. To do the first without the other can lead to pathological behaviors in both the preacher and the listener.

The work of forming concepts is the work of creating an inner world which "is," for us, simply the world. From early childhood we form symbols of the encountered world, immeasurably aided by the acquisition of language, and as Piaget and others show us, we gradually develop the skills of making interpretive models of what is going on out there. Every aspect of the process has given birth to schools of philosophy, but the schools of philosophy come later in the experience of an individual. We begin as naive realists. It is important to us to be able to assume that we know our world, that we see it as it is, with clear eyes, and are not mistaken about it. When we find on some occasion that we are mistaken, and that reality is not what we thought it was, the experience of such failure can touch off deep anxiety. We have what might be called a primitive need to know reality, for survival and therefore for sanity.

It comes as something of a surprise, therefore, to discover how arbitrary much of our supposed knowledge of reality is. We take with equanimity, and even with pleasure, any discovery of error that leads to improved knowledge, but it can produce a certain giddiness to discover that we observe a world of our own constructing rather than the "real" world. When a man leaves naive knowing behind, he enters the confusing sophistications of epistemology, the knowledge problem, a seemingly endless circle of searchings for the proper way to know a world. For many generations we could assume that at least solid objects of ordinary experience were really there and were just about what we thought they were, but even this elementary certainty has been destroyed by the scientific peeling of the onion of matter. We do have, of course, a

74

fairly successful system for representing reality symbolically in our minds, and our survival proves it. But what works for ordinary experience, and fairly well, is not enough for extraordinary experience, and it is the philosophers, the psychologists, the anthropologists, and all who study man, who make themselves obnoxious by forcing us to look at the matter more closely.

Consider, as a way of getting into this tricky situation, the way children begin to learn the art of naming things.[1] We must learn to do a simple, yet mysterious, thing: to recognize that things can be lumped together into classes. As William James put it, man begins to be human when he can say, "Aha, thingumabob again." He recognizes not only the possibility that objects can have a continuing identity, but that two objects may be instances of a common something. Provided with a verbal pigeonhole by an indulgent parent, the child not only names the object, "dog," but subsumes another experience under that category. He may also fit cows and horses under that category, and call them all dogs, but he is on his way, now, to organizing his universe, noting similarities and differences, and making important decisions about how to deal with new experiences in the light of the categories he has available.

J. S. Bruner gave children two words: banana and peach, and asked how they were alike.[2] A third word was then added: potato. How does it differ? How are all three alike? The list went on through meat, milk, water, air, germs, to stones; with the last, the question was: How does it differ? Children at early ages went through quite complex strategies for finding similarities. They ingeniously worked out ways of finding the second and following words similar to the first, or they worked out pairs of similarities, or linked them all in a narrative. But older children found "superordinate concepts," as if they stood back from the cluster and saw through the surface differences to some underlying quality such as "nourishing." The strategies of the younger children were complicated: they were unskilled categorizers. It would seem that a child is impressed by all the details of the object, with a rather admirable concern for its uniqueness. He must learn, we say, to move from those aspects of the object that are "appearances" to those that constitute its abstract "reality." Banana and peach may not *look* alike, but they *are* alike in one or more ways. Life imposes on the growing child the need to develop the skill of categorizing. One hopes that we do not at the same time destroy his wonderful skill at seeing the uniqueness of the object. But without the ability to organize a complex environment in some way, the mind would expire of instant overload.

One can relive in a limited way the child's confusion as he confronts a universe of multiple objects by taking an "object sorting test." [3] Consider the following list of items:

| spoon | orange | violin |
|-------|--------|--------|
| book | button | necktie |
| bottle | hat | cat |
| cigar | string | wheel |
| key | fishhook | ball |

They are obviously a mixed lot and at first glance seem to fall into no natural categories. The task is simply to put together in groups whatever seem to go together. Any number of groups will do. Some objects may seem to stand alone. Some may seem to be candidates for admission to more than one group. There could be a series of solutions to the task, depending on the changing mood of the sorter. Sorting by color, by weight, by use, are possibilities, and psychologists may find it informative to observe whether many categories are used, or only a few. The exercise may seem trivial, but it begins to reveal some of the ways that we bring to the world our assumptions about how it should be organized at more than a trivial level. The objects are seen as taking their places in a social system. Each of them begins to be rich with associations. "Fishhook" reminds us of one world, "violin" of another. For it is not just *objects* that are sorted out and located within a system of meanings. Every aspect of life has its place in a hierarchy of meanings, culminating in those large-scale, all-inclusive statements that make, or are intended to make, sense of the whole system. The objects are found, perhaps in a house, collected there by a family with purposes, behaviors, likes and dislikes. And the family is part of a community that has customs which regulate family life, and industries that provide objects, and a cluster of values that give coloration to every element of the system. And concerning it all, the great questions can be asked: It is good? Why is it there at all? Where did it come from? Where is it going? Who's in charge here?

From the simple objects and their categorization (chairs and tables are "furniture") to the great questions, the process of sense-making moves up a ladder of increasing complexity. The process becomes more *inclusive,* taking in larger and larger clusters of data, and it becomes more *abstract,* requiring the formation of concepts that demand some hard cognitive work. It is easy to see that chairs and tables are "furniture," but with what does "furniture" go, and under what higher category can it be subsumed? (Try linking it with "appliances," to make a new category:

"household goods." But then what?) And the plain fact, as we all know, is that not everyone works his way up the cognitive ladder. Few of us continue after childhood to ask "why?" We may wonder which of two actions is "right," but seldom do we sit down and reflect on the principles by which "rightness" itself is determined. The mental energy required for pushing on toward ultimate questions is unevenly distributed among us. And there are probably matters of intellectual ability to be considered. An aptitude for thinking abstractly can be tested, with suggestive, if not conclusive, results.[4] Given a proverb such as, "Rome wasn't built in a day," one is asked to express the meaning of the proverb in general terms. Answers could range from the (literal) "It took centuries to build that ancient city," to the (abstract) "Great ventures take time." For some, the task comes easily; others clearly have to work at it. There is some evidence, incidentally, that the blind have more difficulty than sighted people with this test, as if vision exercised the mind in some way in the skills of achieving detachment from particulars.

Evidence that the mind needs time to do certain kinds of thinking is presented by work being done on "hesitation," the usually unnoticed pauses in speech which the mind needs for word search, at just those places in the utterance where a difficult idea is to be expressed.[5] The reader of a book can make such pauses for himself, but when he is read to (as by a preacher reading a manuscript sermon) he may need pauses that the reader does not permit him—after all, once the material is written down, the writer has no further problem with the content, and may not be able to recover his sense of where the pauses ought naturally to come. A discourse on difficult subjects, requiring either a special vocabulary or at least a vocabulary not easily activated, is a discourse that puts demands on a listener that are worth our sympathetic attention, for he may need times for processing those sections that tax the mind. When we think of the verbal behavior of a preacher, these findings may suggest that as he carefully writes an eloquent sermon he is unwittingly planning a communication that will demand unusual efforts on the part of his listeners. It is no wonder that they often say that they prefer the conversational sermon delivered from notes.

Since from the psychological point of view the work of thinking abstractly is difficult (and rarely done), it may not be surprising to discover that human life is arranged so that it is largely done for us. The meanings of things, ranging all the way from the names we give to objects to the answers we give to great questions, are provided by the "culture," that accumulation of wisdom about the world that a community retains as its heritage and which it carefully teaches to each new generation. Once learned, it makes philosophical musings unnecessary. One knows that monogamy is right, murder is wrong, kindness is good, cruelty is bad. During the period of socialization, the "why" questions may be asked and the educational system provides teachers trained to give the answers that explain. "Higher" education, at its best, produces an appropriate kind of "why" questioning as a continuing behavior for life ("the unexamined life is not worth living"). But for many people, the availability of trusted, acceptable meanings, together with their natural inability for pursuing abstract questions, combine to make a life characterized by *living within* a meaning system rather than by consciously working out meanings for themselves.

Since it is the acquisition of language that permits the mind to develop the detached life of abstract thought, and to reflect about the world in the absence of immediate sensory inputs, we can find in language a rich storehouse of the varieties of abstract behavior.[6] Furthermore, it is in language that we can find those aspects of the handling of abstractions which are prominent in communication behaviors, and especially in such verbal religious communication as preaching. And since language is only a little less mysterious than man himself, we can only identify a few of its elements.

One of the major functions of language is to record those elements of experience which have been identified as important for the life of the people who speak the language. Arabs must know many words for camels, especially pregnant camels; Eskimos have many words for snow; in the Philippines, there are ninety-two terms for rice. Thus perceptual discrimination requires an extensive lexicon to match the observed detail. A language becomes loaded with words that refer to the particular behaviors of a culture.

There is a larger issue which linguistic usage may raise, and it goes by the name of Benjamin Lee Whorf, although he was not the first to raise the issue.[7] The Whorfian Hypothesis says that since a language emerges within the culture of a certain people, and since their experience of the world is naturally limited, that language can only present a limited view of the universe. However rich it may be in linguistic resources (especially in certain domains), it is capable of expressing only what that culture has experienced.

We dissect nature along lines laid down by our native languages. The categories and types that we isolate from the world of phenomena we do not find there because they stare every observer in the face; on the contrary, the world is presented in a kaleidoscope flux of impressions which has to be organized by our minds—and this means largely by the linguistic systems in our minds. We cut nature up, organize it into concepts, and ascribe significance as we do, largely because we are parties to an agreement to organize it in this way—an agreement that holds throughout our speech community and is codified in the patterns of our language.[8]

This theory of "linguistic relativity," if even partly true, raises the right kind of question, for it turns our attention to the kind of question about the obvious that might never be asked. As Joshua A. Fishman says, in a careful review of Whorf's ideas, "Whorf (like Freud) impugns our objectivity and rationality." [9] Furthermore, if thinking operates with a concealed cultural bias or limitation, it may well be that religious thinking would be peculiarly vulnerable to such effects. Charles F. Hockett says just this: "The impact of inherited linguistic patterns on activities is, in general, *least* important in the most practical contexts and most important in such 'purely verbal' goings-on as story-telling, religion, and philosophizing." [10] It is interesting, even amusing, to learn how many words Arabic has for pregnant camels, but such lexical differences seem to be surface differences, easily overcome when speakers from two linguistic families meet, even if translation must be by complex phrases rather than by the matching of single words. The linguistic relativity hypothesis really pinches, however, if it suggests that one is imprisoned within his language so completely that it governs his perception of the universe and limits what he can know of it.

The question is obviously more than a linguistic one,

but it is language, achieved early in life and provided by the culture in which the child is immersed, which provides him with the essential tool for the unpacking of a universe, and the tool is specific, permitting some things to happen and unable to permit others to happen. If the linguistic tool has unsuspected limitations, clearly we want to know about them. And it may be that these considerations will be useful if they do no more than alert us to the way linguistic habits tilt (if they do not actually control) our thinking in the direction of certain cognitive habits. An important case that will need extensive examination in the immediate future is the common use of the masculine gender in God-talk. It might be noted, also, that in pragmatic, technological, activist America it seems important to speak of the God "who acts in history." We are also quite capable of speaking of the God who "is," the "eternal," the "unchanging," but it is action which our culture values, and this predisposes us to a particular linguistic-cultural-cognitive definition. We worry about such discoverable relativism; Whorf suggests the more drastic notion that our language would make it impossible for us to step cognitively outside our habitual limits of thought. When the preacher speaks of the things of the spirit to people who are naive materialists, it may be that no matter how hard both parties try, the efforts to define spirit-words into materialist terms will always leave certain essential notions untouched. "Let us define our terms," we say, hopefully, but Whorf unsettles us with the suggestion that mutual agreement on definitions might be impossible.

From many investigations into the ways by which people do the hard cognitive work of organizing the experiences of life, let us consider one that presents two quite different conceptualizing styles. Two groups of people were interviewed to get their reports on the disastrous effects of a tornado on their community.[11] One group was of limited education and incomes; the other, college graduates with higher incomes. The two reported in clearly differing coding styles, revealing two ways of looking at life and of organizing their understanding of its meaning.

Members of the first group, the less educated, described the disaster as seen by each person as a narrative of events that were related to his own life. In contrast, the other group adopted various points of view, shifting perspectives and putting themselves in the roles of other participants. Like young children, the first group seemed to be dependent on immediate sensory inputs, and structured their description of events to conform to the experience of personal observation.

Further differences between the cognitive behaviors of the two groups were revealed by their styles of communication. The first, more "concrete" group assumed that the imagery they used—the terms, names, references and the like, would be universally understood by the interviewers, as if their immediate world was simply "reality" itself, shared by everyone. The more "abstract" group provided a variety of clarifying and illustrative additions to their reports, as if they understood that a complex event included dimensions of meaning difficult to assimilate.

As further evidence of a "concrete" style, the first group spoke almost entirely about specific people, and could give little information about groups of people (storekeepers, policemen). In contrast, the other group reported easily on the activities of groups and engaged naturally in the task of classifying the chaotic effects of the disaster.

The differences in cognitive behavior of these two series of interviews may be due to more than the educational factor, but whatever the causes, they illustrate how differently a universe can be observed and organized. For some of us, the immediate details—things and people seen and heard and touched—cluster before us in all their variety. The "larger picture" just does not emerge. For others, these details are collected, but they are laid out upon the table, sorted and arranged; patterns are discovered, similarities are noted, and the collection of data is organized according to large, inclusive ideas.

Sermons, however simple their style or vivid their concrete illustrations, urge the mind toward reflection on larger meanings—the largest meaning of all. For this reason (and there are others) the sermon commonly relies *on cognitive work already done.* It presents the conclusions to which the faith has come, and assumes that they are familiar, and need reinforcement rather than proof. But even this natural strategy can run into difficulties, as a deeper look into the cognitive process may reveal. Operating at that deeper level, as the engineered structures to support our belief system, are our opinions, attitudes, and values, to which all the cognitive life that we have examined so far contributes. Into this structure we must now venture, for that is precisely what a sermon tries to do.

# 7

# Tolerance for Ambiguity: Cognitive Styles

When the preacher stands in the pulpit and looks down (actually, but not metaphorically, we hope) at the congregation, it would be natural in these days of controversy for him to see before him a group of people with strong opinions, so that a significant number of them seems to him to embody a modification of a current adage to read, "My mind is made up; don't confuse me with the sermon!" If a congregation is human, it is composed of people with a complex network of opinions and attitudes about their world. Sooner or later, if he is a preacher worth his salt, he will plan to modify in some way some of those attitudes, and instinctively he knows that when he does, he will be engaged in one of the hardest tasks of his ministry.

It would be absurd to think that when a man accumulates information about his universe, he is simply piling up discrete pieces of information, which are tucked away into a memory bank to be ready for recall. Something more complicated and mysterious than this obviously occurs, for all this "information" settles down into a mix which becomes, in fact, the man himself. It is formed into what we might call his personality; in one sense, he is what he eats, but in a deeper sense, he is what he knows. And while he can remember many things, he could never recall and display that totality of his knowledge which is himself. Any biography or autobiography, however excellent, demonstrates this.

Nevertheless, certain parts of this complex internal mix can be identified. Opinions, attitudes, and values are the cognitively discernable elements of the inner life of the person. The three words have no common meanings for such a discussion as this, but one way of distinguishing among them ranges them in an order of increasing generality and importance. *Opinions* relate to specifics, and are the application of *attitudes,* which are more general, to particular cases. *Attitudes,* then, are rooted in *values,* which are more general still, and probably more enduring and deeply rooted than attitudes. All three words refer to a network of cognitive formations of data about the world, organized to provide ways of understanding it and behaving in it. Chesterton conflated all three when he said that if he were to rent a room, he would want to know his landlady's metaphysics.

It should be added that attitudes (to speak of all three by that single term) are not simply cognitive; since the whole person is to some extent invested in his attitudes, attitudes are emotional as well as cognitive. As one definition says, they are "valenced cognitions," cognitions with an emotional tone. They represent ways of being for or against the world and its encountered elements.

The first thing to be said about attitudes is that they serve an absolutely necessary function for survival.[1] As the codified educated responses a man has ready for encountering the world, they function as his ways of dealing with it on the basis of experience. Like "concepts" or "words" they are the (more complex) tools he retains for recognizing and interpreting the data with which his environment bombards him—more complex because they put together into a pattern the more isolated data that are distinguished by the perceptual process.

Being necessary, they tend to be valued when they are stable. It is important to the organism, as it moves through a changing, varied environment, to be able to recognize and evaluate what's there, to distinguish friend from foe, and rapidly, for there may not be time to deliberate. The process of forming and holding attitudes seems to have kept what we might think of as the operating pattern that was built into it by the way it functioned far back in the early history of reflective man. If our response to environmental events is not genetically programmed, and instead must be worked out by a less automatic system, the perceptual-cognitive system, then it must at least develop an operating efficiency, and this means clear-cut attitudes, ready to be applied as judgments concerning the meaning of events as they are encountered. This explains one aspect of the function of a "culture." Attitudes are psychologically necessary but they are also sociologically necessary. They must be learned. And as they tend to be fixed in a mind so they tend also to be fixed in a culture. A man's opinions may be personal and rather easily changed, but he shares with his fellows a set of attitudes, and these he knows are rooted in the culture that defines for him the values that seem to him unquestionable, universal, and an authentic part of "reality." For both psychological and sociological security, a stable structure of meanings must be available and must seem to have a reasonable degree of trustworthiness and stability.

Stable, and yet open to modification. Remember the parable of the cell. Its ideal existence is defined by a favorable environment in which it operates with a minimum of decisions. (Put that way, it sounds like an ideal existence for what we used to call the tired businessman.) But when the environment changes, any organism that can only operate with a few fixed responses finds itself unable to cope. For the human organism, the complexities of personal and social existence demand the kind of flexibility of response that will permit *learning,* at least in the technological culture of our recent centuries. Our perceptual sensitivities, combined with environmental change and complexity, make it necessary for the individual to learn, to be a man, and to continue to be a man.

Remember not only the cell, but a few things we all know about religion. One way of looking at religion is to consider its function within individual and social life. It serves as a wisdom about living, a plan for living, and living more abundantly, a "way." It not only offers a plan, but (within Christian thought, at least) it must set its plan over against the plans people have adopted, and which range from the higher naturalisms of the best of the secular traditions to the distorted personal plans of natural, sinful man. One function of the preacher is to set the Christian way over against its competitors, and to persuade people to adopt it. And one way to define the problem of preaching is to say that it is an effort to move people to revise their hard-won structuring of the world, their meaning system, or to put it more dramatically, to change what they hang on to in order to keep sane.

Our concern, then, is not only with being right about the plan, but with the way people cling to the plan they already have, and to feel a pastoral concern for their reluctance to change it. Even when they know that it is inadequate, or woefully incomplete, or rapidly disintegrating, some deep, organic body wisdom advises them to keep what they have rather than to fly to evils that they know not of. It is important, therefore, that the preacher know something about the ways that meaning structures are retained. The issue is not *what* a person believes, but *how* he believes it, his believing "style."

A convenient way of opening this large subject is to think of believing behavior as located on a scale ranging from *flexibility* to *rigidity*.[2] What we are locating on the scale is a person's habitual way of processing information presented to him—does he put it at once into a clear-cut category, or does he sometimes permit the data to suggest a modification of the category so that he actually does what we graphically describe as "changing one's mind." It might be noted that we shall not be talking about intelligence, but we do have in mind a structure that can be thought of as deep enough, and enduring enough, to be thought of as a part of one's personality.

Studies of flexibility-rigidity have had a long history, and one chapter of this has been the investigation of the effects of rigidity on perception, some of which we have already noted. One famous experiment revealed the difficulty some children had with perceiving change in a set of drawings in which a dog was gradually changed into a cat; it was as if they clung to the perception that was clear, and were reluctant to accept the new data.[3] Frenkel-Brunswik, who made these studies, related rigidity in children to authoritarian behavior in their parents:

> The requested submission and obedience to parental authority is only one of the many external, rigid and superficial rules which such a child learns . . . dominance-submission, cleanliness-dirtiness, badness-goodness, virtue-vice, masculinity-femininity are some of the dichotomies customarily upheld in the homes of such children.[4]

Such a child, faced with demands at home which he cannot meet, learns to conform to external rules, and finds his defense against the threats of life in obedience to clear, unchangeable structures. He learns, therefore, in his own defense to have a low "tolerance of ambiguity."

Studies in rigidity range from examining the ways rigid personalities perceive, to the opinions they hold, and to the ways they hold them. Classic among these is *The Authoritarian Personality*, published in 1950, a volume in a series entitled "Studies in Prejudice," designed to record basic research stimulated by the anti-Semitism of Nazi Germany (and many other places).[5]

For the rigid person, the environmental bombardment must be met defensively. Budner defines "intolerance of ambiguity" as the tendency to perceive and interpret ambiguous situations as sources of threat, and for him "ambiguity" can be either completely new data (which seems to provide no clues for its interpretation), or an overload of data (too many clues), or contradictory data (which triggers opposing interpretations).[6] Furthermore, he found that intolerance of ambiguity correlated with self-ratings as "conventional," "cautious," "ordinary," and "timid," and with belief in God, attendance at religious services, less wondering about religious meanings, and with idealization of, and submission to, parents! Clustered in that one study are matters that will concern us in the near future.

One way of searching beneath the rigidity-flexibility description of behavior is provided by O. J. Harvey and his colleagues.[7] He locates conceptual behavior on a range that has as its extremes "concreteness" and "abstraction." Concreteness provides an explanation of rigidity by thinking of rigid thinking as closer to immediate perceptual experience. It is more automatic, involving less conceptual activity. Abstract thinking, as the word implies, points to a more extensive, flexibly organized set of concepts at work. One is reminded of the distinction that Piaget demonstrated by the thinking of children capable of conserving quantity, in contrast to their earlier thinking in which the immediate perceptual experience could control and mislead. Harvey's description of the difference is this:

> More concrete functioning is expressed at the behavioral level by high stimulus-response requiredness, the extreme of which could be illustrated by such one-to-one correspondence as that between the stimulus of a light and the toxic response of a moth. More abstract functioning on the other hand, because of a more enriched and complex mediational system and a greater ability to transcend and depart from the immediate and perceptual characteristics of the impingements, results in less absolutism, that is, greater relativism in thought and action.[8]

The descriptions of the typical mental behavior of the "concrete" persons in this research begin to paint a portrait, admittedly of the extreme case, as an aid to identification.

91

Such a person has a "simpler cognitive structure": he tends to make extreme and polarized evaluations of data; he depends on authorities rather than on his own powers of discernment and of judgment; he has a low tolerance for ambiguity; he finds it hard to change his mind, and depends on stereotypes. One summary list of the behaviors of the concrete person reads:

> A higher score on the factor of dictatorialness reflected in such behavioral characteristics as high need for structure, high rule orientation, high dictation of procedure, high frequency of the usage of unexplained rules, high punitiveness, low diversity of activities, and low encouragement of individual responsibility.[9]

The descriptive terms for the constricted, rigid mind have begun to accumulate: simple conceptual structures, black-white evaluations, ethnocentrism, reliance on stereotypes, absolutism—and, as we shall continue to see, superstition, religiosity, and dogmatism. Included or implied in these patterns of behavior are elements of explanation, expressive of an emerging theory to account for them. "Concrete" mental functioning is described as if it were undeveloped, a kind of conceptualizing appropriate to early childhood. More "abstract" behavior engages the conceptual life more fully. And the investigation of these differences suggests strongly that certain kinds of childhood experiences have acted to inhibit possible development.

We turn now to a more theoretical, less tightly woven model for such behaviors, one that moves us closer to an examination of these behaviors in philosophical and religious thinking: the "open-closed" system of Milton Rokeach.

Rokeach and his colleagues published *The Open and Closed Mind* in 1960, as an extension of the investigations reported in *The Authoritarian Personality*.[10] That book had focused on "right authoritarianism," that of the Nazi. It had then been suggested that the same personality characteristics could be found in those who hold leftist views. Rokeach moved beyond this:

> In other words, if our interest is in the scientific study of authoritarianism, we should proceed from right authoritarianism not to a refocus on left authoritarianism, but to the general properties held in common by all forms of authoritarianism.[11]

He intends to study authoritarianism apart from any *content;* in short, to make a study of its *structure.* Furthermore, such studies fall into a larger category—the study of belief systems, which means "each and every belief and disbelief of every sort the person may have built up about the physical and social universe he lives in. We mean it to represent each man's *total* framework for understanding his universe as best he can." [12]

To what extent would it be meaningful to speak of structural properties that tie together a person's ideological, conceptual, perceptual, and esthetic systems? Is it possible to say that the extent to which a person's belief system is open or closed is a generalized state of mind which will reveal itself in his politics and religion, the way he goes about solving intellectual problems, the way he works with perceptual materials, and the way he reacts to unorthodox musical compositions? [13]

When the baby begins to touch, taste, and in other ways inspect his environment, he begins the process which moves from muscle and nerve, and the programming of the genetic codes, to metaphysics, religion, and the dance of the ultimates. The process has a style for which his terms "open" and "closed" (used, it should be noted, in a somewhat special way) correspond to the terms "flexible" and "rigid."

For our purposes, the most useful portion of Rokeach's analysis is his three-part division of beliefs on a dimension extending from "central" beliefs to "peripheral" beliefs.

Beliefs may be "central": that is, beliefs about the physical universe, about human nature, about myself—about *reality*. He calls such beliefs "primitive," and says, "One definition of primitive belief is any belief that virtually everyone is believed to have also." [14] In one's central belief region will be located the conventional metaphysical wisdom of one's day.

The "intermediate" region (of the central-peripheral dimension) is the set of beliefs one has about *authority*, the sources from which most beliefs are derived. For much of our knowledge, especially new knowledge not included within the central belief region, we depend on sources. There are, however, important variations in the kind of dependence we may have upon our authorities. The intermediate belief region also includes beliefs about people in general, and Rokeach notes that most of our acceptance or rejection of data is, to use his term, "opinionated." That is, we link our attitude toward an opinion with our attitude toward those who hold it, saying "Any intelligent person knows . . ." or "Only a stupid person would think. . . ."

Finally, a "peripheral" belief region includes the beliefs that do not fall into the central or intermediate regions.

These are the great body of beliefs and opinions of varying importance that we know many people do not share with us; they do not have sufficient generality of acceptance to fall into the central belief region.

Within that region of "primitive," basic beliefs about reality, which one assumes everybody holds to be true, a person may be described as "closed" to the extent that the specific content of his primitive beliefs is that the world is a hostile and dangerous place, whereas for the "open" person, the world is generally "friendly." Pessimism about nature, man and self marks the closed person; optimism about these traditional areas of metaphysics marks the person who is open.

Concerning the nature and function of "authority," the closed person needs authorities who are "absolute," clear and firm in their findings, and people who disagree with accepted authorities are rejected. For the open person, authorities are valued more loosely, and disagreement with them or among them is taken less seriously.

That large collection of "peripheral beliefs," which do not qualify for membership among the basic beliefs of the central region, are held by the closed person chiefly because they have the backing of authority, and therefore contradictions among them may not be noticed. They are *psychologically* related rather than *logically* related. For the more open person, peripheral beliefs are, as Rokeach puts it, "in relative communication with each other," and are less the result of blind acceptance of the voice of authority. The open person does more of the work of conceptual decision-making for himself. Many peripheral beliefs are about ambiguous data. A person knows that there is no consensus of conclusions about such data, but the open person leans less heavily upon authorities and puts more trust in his own sorting out of the evidence.

The closed person, who comes through in this system as the most easily described, is revealed as pessimistic and anxious in his central beliefs. The universe is hostile and dangerous; people are not to be trusted; his own self-esteem is low.

> Thus, the more closed the belief-disbelief system, the more do we conceive it to represent, in its totality, a tightly woven network of cognitive defences against anxiety. . . . Indeed, we suggest that in the extreme, the closed system is nothing more than the total network of psychoanalytic defence mechanisms organized together to form a cognitive system and designed to shield a vulnerable mind.[15]

All belief systems, he says, "serve two powerful and conflicting sets of motives at the same time: the need for a cognitive framework to know and to understand and the need to ward off threatening aspects of reality." [16] When reality is threatening, the need to know may be satisfied by authorities, and therefore in the closed system, authorities must be strong, unambiguous, clear, and supportive of other elements in the belief system. Openness, then, becomes "the extent to which the person can receive, evaluate, and act on relevant information received from the outside on its own intrinsic merits, unencumbered by irrelevant factors in the situation arising from within the person or from the outside," such as "unrelated habits, beliefs, and perceptual cues, irrational ego motives, power needs, the need for self-aggrandizement, the need to allay anxiety, and so forth." [17]

It is the closed system that can be most sharply defined,

and clearly it represents a behavior which Rokeach (and his readers, probably) finds undesirable. Yet anyone with a closed mind has the same subjective experience of his cognitive process that the person with an open mind has; it does, after all, satisfy the need to know. And he adds, "the real people we all know have systems that are neither completely open nor completely closed. Furthermore, like the diaphragm on a camera, a system can expand and contract within limits, as conditions vary." [18]

The central belief region in Rokeach's analysis is of special interest to the theologian. Beliefs about "reality," assumed to be universally accepted, so true as to be immune to doubt or contradiction, form a person's metaphysic, his ideas of space, time, causality, substance, together with the emotional valence that determines their value. On his Dogmatism Scale—the instrument he devised for testing for open or closed behavior—closed persons give affirmative responses to these statements:

11. Man on his own is a helpless and miserable creature.
12. Fundamentally, the world we live in is a pretty lonesome place.
13. Most people just don't give a "damn" for others.
23. At times I think I am no good at all.[19]

Discovering the causes that might produce a closed system would be difficult since they probably lie somewhere in childhood, perhaps in unpredictable parental controls, or in an early deprivation of the freedom to explore and to take creative risks. But we seem on firmer ground when we notice that environmental change and uncertainty can move a belief system toward closure. For a person, and perhaps for a culture, there seems to be a level of tolerable uncertainty in the intellectual structures by which the universe is comprehended. In the interplay between security and creativity which must achieve some sort of balance in the human organism's encounters with its environment, the closed person loads the scales on the side of security. For him it is necessary that the interpretive structures by which the world is defined should be clear and distinct, and for the most part unchanging, and expressed for him by an authoritative voice. Like the eye observing the visual permutations of a rotating cube, but maintaining the knowledge that the cubic form remains undistorted, the closed person must automate, as much as possible, his observation of the more complex events of life, and for his own sanity and peace of mind maintain a sense of their stability. In the closed person we have a definition of the pathological philosopher whose capacity to read the changing events of a world in process has become distorted by internal insecurities so that he can no longer keep open the lines of communication between himself and his world.

These studies of closed, concrete behavior are given a special importance to us by the possibility that the closed person tends to seek out religion and to find in a church the security, clarity, and moral strictness that he values. A long history of investigation into this matter has accumulated, and Dittes testifies to the unsatisfactory state of this research.[20] Much of it equates "religious" with "church-going" and fails to distinguish among the varieties of religious belief and expression. For our purposes it is enough to assume that in most congregations a significant number of closed minds will turn up, and we need not worry about whether such minds cluster in churches more than in other institutions. In recent years especially, a diffuse environmental threat, built up by rapid cultural change and intensified by a series of dramatic transformations of social structures, has probably shifted many minds in the direction of closedness.

The closed mind shows in various ways its insecurity. Troubled by ambiguity, novelty, confusion, and uncertainty, it turns to strong authorities for reassurance and guidance. In its primitive beliefs it finds the universe to be threatening, and man and nature are evil. To such a mind, the contemporary decline of authorities and institutions compounds the difficulties. An authority must pass two tests. It must have *strength* (clarity, simplicity, definiteness) and *pessimism* (with a focus on sin, guilt, and punishment). When the churches, the supposed havens of order and security, called for social reform and liturgical change in a time of cultural transition, many people experienced a sense of outrage. Not surprisingly, conservative churches flourished. Yet many a "liberal" churchman, who might be put off by the old-time religion, nevertheless may feel some degree of metaphysical anxiety and he may welcome stability and structure where it can be found.

Let us put a case in a clear, simple, structured form (as a relief from our own anxieties). Consider a congregation made up of Rokeach's closed minds. The preacher enters the pulpit, as the authoritative person taking the authoritative place. He speaks of God's goodness, and of His love for the good world that he loves, and of His forgiveness for all people, and the sermon suggests that the congregation learn to see the emerging needs and values of the new culture, and get out and join the action. The preacher speaks, however, to people who know that the world is dangerous and bad and that people are evil and that the old ways are familiar, safe, and only rejected by criminals and troublemakers. As the preacher speaks, his "authority" leaks rapidly away; he unfits himself, in the eyes of the people, to speak for the tradition. What is Good News to the preacher is bad news to the congregation. At a deep, subcognitive level they know he is wrong. The wrongness seems to be at the level of ideas, but the problem lies deeper than that. It lies in differing ways that preacher and congregation do their thinking, and which do indeed affect the results of the thinking. But to negotiate at the level of ideas only is to miss the mark.

For the preacher, responsible for controlling the preaching event, the issue may be put in this way: How can he speak so that he enables the listener to hear that which he is unable to hear? How can the preacher devise a metacommunication strategy which will make communication possible?

The general difficulty we all have in building the more abstract levels of our metaphysical structures can be given a pathological intensity if our internal security is weak, or environmental threat is more than we can deal with. If such pathologies can seem to demand of the preacher both forms and contents of preaching that he knows to be illicit, as untrue to the gospel or inappropriate to his function as preacher, then the preacher must include in his repertory of homiletical skills one which might be termed therapeutic. Whenever he ventures to lead people into reflection upon important matters, his discourse may need to include a compassionate attention to the distress that such reflection can cause, and an informed attention to ways of helping people be healed of their cognitive anxieties. The preacher may not be able to heal the person in depth, but he can give therapeutic attention to the distress that the homiletical event may be producing in many listeners.

# 8

# Cognitive Tuning: Preaching in a New Key

It was in 1921 that the second edition of Barth's commentary on Romans was published, and a major voice of Protestant theology began to be heard.[1] It would be hard to overestimate the influence of Karl Barth, but it would be safe to say that for about half a century he was for many students of theology the chief influence on their thinking. And not only on their theological thinking, for since preaching was of great importance to Barth, his theology defined for many preachers their strategy and rationale of preaching, and it has defined the theory which has been used to justify the form and content of the ministry of the Word within the eucharist.

Nothing could be more natural as a justification of the sermon and as description of its nature, for Barth reaffirms the tradition that says that God speaks through scripture and through the preacher, making the preaching event a divine action that breaks in upon man's futile round of philosophical speculations and brings what man could never discover on his own. Such a theory of preaching assumes, and even celebrates, the gap between human knowledge and revealed knowledge.

> Preaching is the Word of God which he himself has spoken; but he makes use, according to his good pleasure, of the ministry of a man who speaks to his fellowmen, in God's name, by means of a passage of Scripture. Such a man fulfills the vocation to which the Church has called him, and through his ministry, the Church is obedient to the mission entrusted to her.[2]

Elaborating on this, Barth goes on to say:

> The starting point is the fact that God wills to reveal himself; he himself bears witness to his Revelation; he has effected it and will effect it. Thus preaching takes place in obedience, by listening to the will of God. This is the process in which the preacher is involved, which constitutes part of his life and controls the content as well as the form of his preaching. Preaching is not a neutral activity, nor yet a joint action by two collaborators. It is the exercise of sovereign power on the part of God and obedience on the part of man.
>
> Only when preaching is controlled by this relationship can it be regarded as "kerygma," that is, as news proclaimed by a herald who thereby fulfills his function.[3]

This might be called a "high" doctrine of preaching, stressing the unique, given quality of revelation, the derived, but nevertheless great, authority of the preacher and giving to the act of preaching a numinous possibility. The miracle of revelation can happen again in the hearing of sermons if the preacher is faithful to his commission.

There are many church people, preacher and listener alike, for whom such a theory of preaching seems natural and inevitable, given the Christian understanding of God and the uniqueness of the incarnation. Nevertheless, just as Barthian theology itself has in recent years lost much of its persuasiveness, this theory has begun to suffer the death of a thousand qualifications. For preachers, it has so many advantages that it is modified only with reluctance, but modification becomes necessary. It is haunted by the ghosts of many unanswered questions concerning the authority of scriptures. It raises worrisome questions about mistaking man's voice for God's voice. It is subtly undermined by the scientific and democratic tradition that knows the importance of cooperative searching for truth, and which distrusts any claim to infallibility. At its worst, it seems to try to solve the major metaphysical problems of man by an act of spiritual violence, as if it hoped to override the contemporary search for truth by fiat.

If preaching strategies and theories were thought of as located on a range or spectrum, we could think of this high doctrine of preaching as defining one extreme, with an alternative doctrine at the opposite end of the spectrum, and this we might call, in mild opposition to the first, or Barthian, theory, "apologetical." It is a theory of preaching that stresses the arts of reconciliation, finding in the world points of contact with the biblical revelation. One thinks of the long tradition of the free churches as exemplars of this theory, and the liberal theology that valued man's efforts in religious thinking, and which was the target for Barth's revelational theology. Behind such preaching was the long, hopeful enterprise of natural theology, which in its post-Thomistic forms usually meant the teleological argument, sustained by the findings of science. It was a gallant tradition, and it flourished long past the deadly analysis of it by David Hume. It was Charles Gore who said that the nineteenth century was built on the twin pillars of the Bible and the teleological argument, and at the end of the century, both were destroyed. Biblical criticism had eroded the authority of the Bible, and the critiques of Hume and others had caught up with the arguments for the existence of God.

One might ponder the fact that for a considerable number of preachers today, the justification for preaching is based upon a combination of these two homiletical doctrines, the one stressing revelation and scripture, and the other stressing apologetics and reason, and with Gore's comment in mind, reflect on the possibility that both are inadequate. The sermon is closely tied to scripture, and both preacher and congregation often keep in uneasy uncertainty the question of how much of what is said is truly the Word of God. As the ordained man, given the right to interpret the Word, the preacher speaks with authority, but clearly the congregation retains some sort of listener's rights, and shares the responsibility with the preacher of discerning God's Word in the words of the preaching man.

What strategy for preaching can be devised which might hope to avoid on the one hand an illicit dependence on God's miraculous rescuing of preacher and congregation from the problem of how to hear only God's Word, and on the other a naive attempt to reconstruct the gospel out of an adroit compilation of current earthly wisdom? Our effort to do this will be based on our examination of the ways by which a man assembles his larger theories about his universe. We shall consider the sermon as designed to assist the listener to do a difficult thing—to relate gospel and life by moving in that area where none of us moves easily, the area where philosophies and theologies operate in us. Our view of the sermon will consider it as a human behavior of great complexity, with the hope of making possible the results anticipated by both the major strategies that we have just briefly identified.

Let us begin by making a working assumption, putting it in a somewhat exaggerated form as a way of sharpening our perception of it. Let us assume that reflection on the deeper meanings of life, difficult for most people in the best of circumstances, is in our day especially difficult. We live in a mental climate that systematically unfits us to do that special kind of thinking required for reflection on ultimate meanings. Ours is a culture that lives by proximate causes and operates with proximate purposes. It is a culture of "how" rather than of "why." If it has a philosophy, that philosophy is pragmatism, a philosophy that can draw effective analogies from engineering.

For such a mental climate, encounters with the language of ultimates can be more intoxicating than nourishing. A Sunday service with sermon can constitute a brief, heady moment with God-talk but often the discussion at the coffee hour afterward reveals how much deep confusion has not been dealt with. The institutional results of such a situation are predictable—a strong and growing biblical fundamentalism, immersed in a religion of the past; a fringe group of experimentalists, searching for renewal within the life of the emotions; and a middle group that continues on by habit, finding little that speaks to their condition, and which drifts away bodily or mentally.

A strategy for preaching that takes seriously the contemporary difficulties in the way of comprehending a discourse about ultimates is suggested to us by a missionary to a culture which has lost its ancient religious tradition and in accepting Western technology has become the victim of its non- (or anti-) metaphysical character. The culture is that of Japan, and the missionary is the Jesuit, Alphonse Nebreda.[4]

In conversations with Japanese non-Christians, Nebreda found that any presentation of the gospel produced incomprehension. The difference between the cognitive systems of the Japanese and of the Christians was simply too great. Greek and Hebraic concepts could no longer be presupposed. Nebreda devised, therefore, a communication strategy for his missionary work which he called "pre-kerygmatic." *Before the kerygma can be presented, the way must be prepared for it.* Pre-kerygmatic work activates the basic human questions about man and his world and strives to find a common ground, an initial agreement on the great questions of life. For Nebreda, raised in the Thomistic tradition, the pre-kerygmatic task was a matter of applied natural theology.

In the Catholic tradition, theology had always been thought of as coming in two "volumes," natural theology and revealed theology. Natural theology prepared the way for revealed theology and was essential to its existence. It has been the decline of natural theology, the "sick man of Europe," [5] that has resulted in much of our present theological weakness, and it is the sermon that throws this weakness into high relief. And as Barthianism (if not Barth himself) reacted against the weaknesses of nineteenth-century natural theology, and formed a strategy for preaching based on the rejection of the apologetical approach, so preaching in the Barthian mode emphasized the kerygma, as if no viable apologetic approaches were trustworthy. We seek, therefore, a new apologetical mode, and adopt Nebreda's term "pre-kerygmatic," and consider it as moving at the level of natural theology, but with the aid of insights into the cognitive process derived from the study of human communication processes, to prepare the mind to understand revealed theology. Until the pre-kerygmatic work is done, the kerygma can be heard but not understood. It lodges in the mind of the listener as somehow familiar, but as detached from the structures by which he makes sense of reality. And the hearing of it can produce a strange response, shot through with feelings of guilt and despair. To put the matter in paradoxical terms, if we want to preach the gospel, we must preach *not the gospel, but preparation for the gospel.*

An illuminating way of describing the two volumes, natural and revealed theology, was popular as late as the seventeenth century. Natural theology is found in the creation, the first great volume that God wrote, and scripture is God's second volume, completing the theme of the first by adding the special truths of redemption. For some, the difference was not between "natural" and "revealed," but between "general revelation" and "special revelation"; in nature, God revealed his will for man by setting forth the structures of life and by planting in man a hunger for ultimate truth and for the fullness of life. It is in the rapid decline of our sense of the universe as a "creation" that we can locate an important part of the problem of contemporary religious thinking. When preaching is at its most ineffective, it is often because the sermon is designed to express the gospel in the summary and abstract terms of theology, as if such a presentation of the distilled essence of the faith would be most true to the command to "preach the gospel," and would serve to guarantee that the voice of God would be predominant over the voice of man. But it is not self-evident that when God speaks, he speaks the abstract language of theology.[6]

Pre-kerygmatic preaching would take as its basic material, and perhaps even its text, the creation. It assumes that only the creation is common to us all, to all cultures and to all degrees of religious interest within a culture. It views creation as revealing, and finds gospel within it, enough to build on. One model for such pre-kerygmatic preaching can be found in drama.

Drama, including cinema, opera, mime, and other forms of theater, has important parallels to the liturgical event and the preaching that occurs within it. A play (excluding plays that simply enact an ideology in a didactic way) selects a portion of the creation and unfolds it, working hard to maintain accuracy in its development of the bit of reality chosen, and to excite the audience to perceive more and more meaning in it. The art of the playwright is tested by his ability to select a luminous piece of reality, so that the natural or realistic unfolding of it does indeed stir the philosophical imagination of the observer. It is "natural" in that the unfolding seems to proceed by a momentum appropriate to the material. The bit of reality chosen thus functions as sacraments do, becoming an enacted symbol productive of meanings. The setting helps to keep the process concentrated. House lights dim, the attention of the audience is controlled and directed, and the time available is limited. And it is important to note that the audience is permitted a degree of freedom; although the play moves toward a resolution intended by the playwright, the audience enjoys a shock of recognition as it draws its own conclusions, and the better the play, the more various the conclusions.

Nearly all these elements of theater would be woven into pre-kerygmatic sermons. The selection of the appropriate bit of reality as "subject," the brief, focused, liturgically controlled occasion, the freedom of the listener to discover meaning for himself, and the stimulation of the listener's imagination to find deeper and deeper levels of significance —all these elements would determine the content of such preaching. One way of distinguishing pre-kerygmatic preaching from other kinds is by the function of the "illustration." Ordinarily, an abstract idea is brought home to the congregation by an illustration from human experience; idea is primary, illustration is secondary. In pre-kerygmatic preaching the illustration *is* the sermon; the illustration, extended and given a dramatic life of its own, is primary, and the ideas generated by it are secondary.

The parallel between pre-kerygmatic preaching and theater breaks down at one important point. The playwright is free to move an audience toward any meaning he wishes, or to leave the play open-ended, or to stimulate reflections of several kinds. The pre-kerygmatic sermon is preached by a Christian to Christians; it is, after all, pre-*kerygmatic*. The preacher, speaking from the vantage point of the faith, holds a particular view of creation, and this governs his selection of material and his treatment of it. He would rarely be content simply to be stimulating, or to provoke something like a free classroom discussion of possible meanings. He returns the listener to the data of life, but he hopes to reveal it for what it is. Yet if he distorts the data to fit his doctrine, his sermon is not in fact pre-kerygmatic, for pre-kerygmatic preaching stands or falls on its being true to reality. He must give to the creation the same exegetical care that he would give a passage of scripture. If his theme is the odd pairing of love and hate, he must know enough about this bit of psychological data to win the respectful assent of the listener, whose first response should be an excited sense of discovery at the level of human nature itself, to which the further insights of the gospel come as further discoveries about the real.

It may be added that a pre-kerygmatic sermon might well begin with a text from scripture and at some point, perhaps at the end, become frankly theological. All sorts of variations of method are as possible with this as with any kind of preaching. What is crucial is the engagement of the sermon in the data of creation, as that which the sermon is "about."

Such preaching moves at the level of an interesting piece of reality, probably of human experience, and this means that unlike systematic theology or formal philosophy, it does not move at the level of organized cognitive structures. It is not, that is, like an argument which presents an opinion or attitude over against an alternative view. Consider how a good play "works" on us. The curtain rises to reveal a living room, and soon people are moving about, a situation begins to emerge, emotions come to the surface, a conflict shapes up. We are free to respond with whatever natural reactions we came with, and at first we see the play much as we see life, screening it through our relatively fixed information processing equipment. Then something like a common experience is generated, and when the play is a good one, the action bites deeper into our structures and forces us to *rethink the data being presented.* No one has told us that we were wrong, and no one is now telling us what we ought to think. But we experience the rare and exciting moment of revising our ordinary operating notions about life, free to do so in the enclosed safety of the theater, and within the protected limits set by the play.

The significance of this procedure for pre-kerygmatic preaching is that it gives us a model of a nonadversary method for enabling a person to revise just those cognitive structures that are most tightly woven. Preaching has strong overtones of being an adversary action, given by the authoritative person of the preacher and the very place and structure of the pulpit a dictatorial quality which is either resented by the strong or unfortunately cherished by the weak. But the preacher should not preach like a lord chancellor. Preaching is essentially a pastoral action. Like pastoral counseling, it is intended to help the person to discover the gospel for himself, and to make it his own, and the obedient acceptance of an imposed faith is simply destructive of that possibility.

Pre-kerygmatic preaching can be thought of as a strategy for bridging cultural and linguistic gaps, but it may have its greatest usefulness as a way of speaking to Rokeach's closed mind. The closed person has an unhealthy dependence upon authorities; he wants them to tell him what to think, and he expects an authority to speak with clarity, simplicity, and power. One might think that only a simple kerygmatic sermon, full of clear teachings and strict moral advice would speak to such a mind. The key to such a mind, however, is that central area of "primitive" beliefs which Rokeach finds to be essentially anxious and pessimistic. As long as the primitive beliefs remain untouched, discourse at the level of a commentary on current affairs, or any interpretive discourse applying the gospel to life, must conform to the demands of the primitive beliefs about human nature and the external universe. How can the

Good News of God's loving forgiveness and providential care be heard if it contradicts beliefs that it is assumed everyone holds to be true?

Clearly the closed mind is highly resistant to direct argument. Even the exposition of contradictions within its belief system does not produce modifications within it, for the belief system is not logically but psychologically structured. Beliefs are held not because they are true but because a respected authority has asserted them. Rokeach speaks of the "party line" behavior in which contradictory beliefs are never brought into logical confrontation and are held in separate compartments.

A radically closed mind would probably yield only to intensive therapeutic treatment, if at all. But "closedness," as a cognitive pattern in which we all share, at least from time to time or when certain sensitive domains are touched upon, may possibly be encouraged toward openness if the beliefs in the primitive area can be affected. It is the special virtue of pre-kerygmatic preaching which begins with the creation, and which follows the model of theater, that it introduces living data from some aspect of life with at first a certain neutrality. Postponing any commentary, such preaching might engage the listener in a recognition of the data, in as much richness of detail as possible, with the hope that he might see a bit of life for himself, for the first time. Perhaps the preacher might not expect his sermons to dig very deeply into life and its meanings, lest he trigger an awaiting pessimistic verdict about "life." The key to the procedure is to avoid threat, and to avoid threat by avoiding the presentation of abstract summary statements, for that is where the cognitive system is rigid.

For open and closed alike, the ambiguities of the contemporary environment and the hazards of contemporary existence place upon the church, and therefore upon the preacher, the necessity of providing for people a renewed awareness of the sources of security. At such a time the false securities will rush in if there is nothing better available. There seems to be at present a tendency to seek security in intense emotional experience. In earlier times, it was understood that God was in charge of things, and any temporary dislocations would eventually be brought into order again by divine action. For our generation, many of those who believe in God find him to be in charge of personal matters rather than cosmic affairs. The obvious thing to say, and it is probably partly true, is that as man has become more powerful, God's function as the determiner of security has weakened. If man now begins to lose confidence in himself, to whom can he turn?

At such a time, it is oddly threatening to be reminded of the ancient traditions; they can sound like the examination answers that we failed to give.

Paul Matussek has written a perceptive essay entitled, "The Function of the Sermon with Regard to Repressed Unbelief in the Believer," in a collection of essays edited by Karl Rahner, with the title *The Pastoral Approach to Atheism*.[7] He notes that many nominal Christians profess belief and attend church, but in life they behave without reference to their formal expressions of faith. When the faith of the church is proclaimed, any latent unbelief of the listener is repressed, but it persists as an unrecognized, diffuse sense of the unlikeliness of the possibility of God's existence and effectiveness in the world that seems to lie outside the bounds of legitimate confession of doubt. I can admit that I doubt, but I dare not admit that the whole enterprise may be untrue.

Clearly not all such unbelief is repressed; churches

contain their vocal village atheists, and even clergy can courageously raise the truth question in radical form. But the usual appeal, if the issue is raised, is to the miracles, as revelation, incarnation, resurrection. As Barth said, "The fixed point from which all preaching starts is the fact that God has revealed himself, and this means that the Word has become flesh; God has assumed human nature; in Christ he has taken on himself fallen man." [8] Far into the age of secularism, the church takes belief as the norm, and belief that is formulated in metaphysical terms difficult for this age to grasp. It would be natural if that were to produce nominal acceptance of doctrines of transcendence, together with repressed unbelief, in many who would welcome the exposure and resolution of the contradiction.

It might be possible that further explorations into the potential of pre-kerygmatic preaching could produce sermons that could speak to such repressed unbelief. Such sermons might introduce believers to an examination of the ways that the religious impulse operates in man, giving special attention to the great events of life that awaken the imagination, and that over the ages have been the substance from which myth is formed. Pre-kerygmatic theology might well look like a "general theory of religion," shaped so that the unbeliever that lives in contemporary man might be enabled to generate as if from a point of basic origin a religion which could become, in its proper time, ready to hear the gospel, and to complete its speculations with truth greater than its wildest hopes.

In 1942 a book was published that celebrated the emergence of a new era in philosophy: *Philosophy in a New Key,* by Susanne Langer.[9] The author spoke of the importance to philosophy of asking the right questions. "A philosophy is characterized more by the *formulation* of its problems than by its solution of them. Its answers establish an edifice of facts; but its questions make the frame in which its picture of facts is plotted." [10] The new question for philosophy in the twentieth century, the "new key" into which its perennial questions may be creatively transposed, Dr. Langer defined by "the fundamental notion of symbolization—mystical, practical, or mathematical . . ."

> In it lies a new conception of "mentality," that may illumine questions of life and consciousness, instead of obscuring them as traditional "scientific methods" have done. If it is indeed a generative idea, it will beget tangible methods of its own, to free the deadlocked paradoxes of mind and body, reason and impulse, autonomy and law, and will overcome the checkmated arguments of an earlier age by discarding their very idiom and shaping their equivalents in more significant phrases.[11]

Man is the creature who represents his world symbolically, capable of bringing the immediate stimulus or the instinctive demand into the openness of consciousness. She found that the philosophical preoccupation with symbols has moved along two distinct courses. One has been that of logic and the theory of knowledge. "The other takes us in the opposite direction—to psychiatry, the study of emotions, religion, fantasy, and everything but knowledge. Yet in both we have a central theme: the *human response,* as a constructive, not a passive thing." [12]

For theology, and especially for natural theology, Dr. Langer's new key seems indeed to be a generative idea, and while the theologian may wince a little at seeing religion linked (again) with fantasy in a category that excludes "knowledge," he hears a reverberation between symbolization, the new key for philosophy, and a possible new key for theology. For like philosophy, theology is the extreme and most complex example of a process characteristic of all life: the absorbing of information by the organism from its environment, making sense of it by means of whatever information processing ability it has learned, and searching for new data, for the purpose of maintaining and enriching its life and of coming to ultimate conclusions about its meaning. It makes the assumption, so absurd at first hearing, that the earliest tentative graspings of the infant may be thought of as of a piece with the speculations of a metaphysician and the meditative prayer of a saint. In harmony with the new key for philosophy, the new key for theology (and for the pre-kerygmatic preaching that links the two) takes religious thinking to be a constructive human response to reality.

Theology, like philosophy itself, has been caught in circular arguments and exhausted questions. Perhaps the new life it needs may be found in the examination of the process by which any and all theologies are formed: man, thinking, with carefulness and reverence, about those matters that we commonly call "religious." The new key for preaching is to be found in "religion," man's information search for ultimates, the necessary pre-kerygmatic discipline which (to use Tillich's word) establishes the correlation between life and gospel. T. Patrick Burke, contributing an essay to *Searching in the Syntax of Things,* states as his thesis: "From now on theological questions can be usefully asked only within the framework of the study of the general phenomenon of religion." [13] It is there that we observe man's explorations into the great questions: the meaning of suffering, the varieties of love, the structures of community, the goals to work for. The dislocation between the theological forms of the inherited

Christian tradition and the shaking structures of meaning of our secularized culture send us back to the elementary forms of the religious life, to borrow Durkheim's luminous phrase. We preach to primitive men and women, for whom the rote acceptance of great answers can bring no authentic relief until the great questions have been asked. Set within the framework of the liturgy, surrounded by the Word, secure within the community of trust, guided by the man of faith, the sermon event may be rediscovered as an event in which the people of this fragile planet may begin to understand how meanings may be found, and may begin to see themselves as the people of God.

# Notes

## 1. On Receiving Messages from the Universe

1. As an introduction to "human communication theory," a good beginning would be: Frank E. X. Dance, *Human Communication Theory* (New York: Holt, Rinehart & Winston, 1967). It has extensive bibliographies. A classic work is Colin Cherry, *On Human Communication* (Cambridge, Mass.: M.I.T. Press, 1957). The general article by Ray L. Birdwhistell in the *International Encyclopedia of the Social Sciences*, Vol. 3 (New York: Macmillan, 1968) opens that great resource to many aspects of the subject.

## 2. From Source to Destination

1. Wiener's book was published by M.I.T. Press and John Wiley in 1948; 2d edition, M.I.T. Press, 1961. An article by Wiener, "Cybernetics," adapted from the book, was published in *Scientific American*, 197 (1948), pp. 14–18. Copyright © 1948 by Scientific American, Inc. All rights reserved. Reprinted in Alfred G. Smith, ed., *Communication and Culture* (New York: Holt, Rinehart & Winston, 1966), pp. 25–35.

2. From the *Scientific American* article, in Smith, op. cit., p. 25.

3. "Pragmatism" appeared as the title of James' book in 1907, with the subtitle, "A New Name for Some Old Ways of Thinking." James says that the word was introduced by Charles Peirce in 1878.

4. For the mathematical theory, see Colin Cherry, *On Human Communication* (Cambridge, Mass.: M.I.T. Press, 1957), chap. 2, section 2. This and an article by Anatol Rapaport, "What Is Information?"

which originally appeared in *ETC,* 10 (1935), pp. 247–60, will both be found in Smith, op. cit., pp. 35–55.

5. The study by R. L. Dahling is entitled "Shannon's Information Theory: The Spread of an Idea." It appeared in Elihu Katz, *Studies in the Utilization of the Behavioral Sciences,* Vol. 2 (Stanford, Calif.: Stanford University Press, 1962), pp. 119–39.

6. L. N. Ridenour, R. R. Shaw, and A. G. Hill, *Bibliography in an Age of Science* (Urbana, Ill.: University of Illinois Press, 1953).

7. *Information Theory in Biology* (Urbana, Ill.: University of Illinois Press, 1953).

8. Henry Quastler, ed., *Information Theory in Psychology* (Chicago: Free Press, 1955).

9. *Psycholinguistics: A Survey of Theory and Practice* (Bloomington, Ind.: Indiana University Press, 1954). It was reprinted in 1967 with "A Survey of Psycholinguistic Research, 1954–1964," by A. Richard Diebold, together with "The Psychologists," by George A. Miller.

10. As an entrance into the vast literature concerning mass communication, see *Mass Communication: A Research Bibliography,* ed. Donald A. Hansen and J. Herschel Parsons (Berkeley, Calif.: Glendessary Press, 1968).

11. Harley C. Shands, "Outline of a General Theory of Human Communication," *Communication Concepts and Perspectives,* ed. Lee Thayer (New York: Spartan Books, 1967), p. 99. Used by permission of United Publishing Corporation.

12. Colin Cherry, "The Communication of Information," *American Scientist,* 40 (1952), pp. 640–63; used by permission. Reprinted in Smith, op. cit., p. 36.


### 3. From Preacher to Listener

1. Claude Shannon, "A Mathematical Theory of Communication," *The Bell Telephone Technical Journal,* 27 (1948), pp. 379–423, 623–56. The model is given on p. 381. Oddly enough, the "channel" box in the diagram is not labeled. The diagram is given in a slightly modified form by Warren Weaver in "The Mathematics of Communication," *Scientific American,* 181 (1949), pp. 11–15; reprinted in Alfred G. Smith, ed., *Communication and Culture* (New York: Holt, Rinehart & Winston, 1966), p. 17.

2. A useful historical sketch of communication models is given by

F. C. Johnson and G. R. Klare, "General Models of Communication Research: A Survey of the Developments of a Decade," *Journal of Communication*, 11 (1961), pp. 13–26, 45.

3. Robert E. Mueller, *The Science of Art* (New York: John Day, 1967), pp. 30–31. Used by permission of The John Day Company, Inc.

## 4. From Data to Symbol: Models of Universes

1. *The Scientific American*, 223 (1970), p. 44. The photograph was taken by Elso S. Barghoorn of Harvard University.

2. A film of the life of the cell similar to our scenario (its source, in fact!) is "Life and Death of a Cell," produced by the University of California.

3. We borrow the diagram, modified for our use, from its reproduction in Albert E. Finholt, "A Society Shaped by Science," *Dialog*, 5 (1966), p. 268. The diagram appears, in more than one form, in *The Nature of Physical Reality* by Henry Margenau (New York: McGraw-Hill, 1950), pp. 85, 106. For Margenau, the "P-plane" is the realm of nature, and is variously called "P-plane," "P-field," and simply "Nature" (and lettered "N").

4. For Brunswik's ideas, see Egon Brunswik, "Scope and Aspects of the Cognitive Problem," *Contemporary Approaches to Cognition* (Cambridge, Mass.: Harvard University Press, 1957).

5. A review of contemporary theories concerning "abstraction" is given by Anatol Pikas, *Abstraction and Concept Formation* (Cambridge, Mass.: Harvard University Press, 1966).

6. The literature on concept formation is extensive. To keep up with it, see the *Annual Review of Psychology*. Especially useful is J. S. Bruner, J. J. Goodnow, and G. A. Austin, *A Study of Thinking* (New York: John Wiley & Sons, 1956).

7. Andre Godin, in *Lumen Vitae Studies in the Psychology of Religion*, IV (Brussels, 1967).

## 5. How to Carve Up a Universe: Perception

1. The best guide to Piaget is his own work, especially a recent summary of his ideas: Jean Piaget and Bärbel Inhelder, *The Psychology of the Child* (New York: Basic Books, 1969). The major study is by J. H. Flavell, *The Developmental Psychology of Jean Piaget* (New York: Van Nostrand, 1963). A more simple approach is by M. Brearley and E. Hitchfield, *A Guide to Reading Piaget* (New York: Schocken, 1967)

in paperback. Piaget's ideas have been applied to Christian education by Ronald Goldman, *Religious Thinking from Childhood to Adolescence* (New York: Seabury Press, 1964) and *Readiness for Religion* (New York: Seabury Press, 1965). Consult *Paperback Books in Print* for Piaget's own works.

2. Piaget and Inhelder, *The Psychology of the Child*, translated from the French by Helen Weaver. © 1969 by Basic Books, Inc., Publishers, New York, p. 3. © 1966 by Presses Universitaires de France. Used by permission.

3. Ibid., p. 4.

4. Ibid., p. 13.

5. Ibid., p. 15.

6. Jean Piaget, *The Construction of Reality in the Child* (New York: Basic Books, 1954).

7. Piaget and Inhelder, op. cit., p. 51.

8. Eric Lenneberg, *The Biological Foundation of Language* (New York: John Wiley & Sons, 1967). The quotation is from his article, "A Biological Perspective of Language," *New Directions in the Study of Language* (Cambridge, Mass.: M.I.T. Press, 1964), p. 66, which he edited.

9. Piaget and Inhelder, op. cit., pp. 96ff.

10. Ibid., p. 98.

11. Ibid., p. 131.

12. Ibid., p. 132.

13. A convenient collection of major philosophical positions is provided by *Perception and the External World*, ed. R. J. Hirst (New York: Macmillan, 1965).

14. An attractive and readable account of perception is given by the general textbook by Peter H. Lindsay and Donald A. Norman, *Human Information Processing* (New York: Academic Press, 1972).

15. For the McGill experiments, see W. Heron, "Cognitive and Physiological Effects of Perceptual Isolation," *Sensory Deprivation*, ed. P. Solomon et al. (Cambridge, Mass.: Harvard University Press, 1961).

16. R. W. Brown and E. H. Lenneberg, "A Study in Language and Cognition," *Journal of Abnormal Social Psychology*, 49 (1954), pp. 454–62.

17. George A. Miller, "The Magical Number Seven, Plus or Minus Two: Some Limits on Our Capacity for Processing Information," *Psychological Review*, 63 (1956), pp. 81–97.

18. For the "cocktail party" phenomenon, see Colin Cherry, *On Human Communication* (Cambridge, Mass.: M.I.T. Press, 1957), pp. 27ff., and his references, especially to his own work. Also D. E. Broadbent, *Perception and Communication* (New York: Pergamon Press, 1958), especially chap. 2 and his article in Alfred G. Smith, ed., *Communication and Culture* (New York: Holt, Rinehart & Winston, 1966), chap. 26.

19. N. Moray, "Attention in Dichotic Listening: Affective Cues and the Influences of Instruction," *Quarterly Journal of Experimental Psychology*, 11 (1959), pp. 56–60. Cited by Anne Treisman in *New Horizons in Psychology*, ed. Brian M. Foss (Baltimore, Md.: Penguin, 1966), p. 109.

20. Memory has received continuing attention, with a burst of new studies recently. See chaps. 8 through 12 in Lindsay and Norman, op. cit., and the readings suggested there, for an excellent introduction to memory and forgetting.

21. For visual perception, in addition to Lindsay and Norman, op. cit., chaps. 1 through 5, there is R. L. Gregory, *Eye and Brain* (New York: McGraw-Hill, 1966). M. D. Vernon's collection, *Experiments in Visual Perception* (Baltimore, Md.: Penguin, 1966) and Julian E. Hochberg, *Perception* (Englewood Cliffs, N.J.: Prentice-Hall, 1964) are easily available.

22. R. L. Gregory, *The Intelligent Eye* (New York: McGraw-Hill, 1970); Rudolph Arnheim, *Visual Thinking* (Berkeley, Calif.: Univeristy of California Press, 1971). Both books are available in paperback. Gregory's book is a delight and includes two-color viewers to use with experiments in three-dimensional vision, and other goodies.

23. Arnheim, op. cit., p. 27.

24. There are many fascinating studies of visual illusions, and the references concerning visual perception will usually include them, especially by Gregory.

25. The Necker cube dates from the work of L. A. Necker in 1832: "Observations on Some Remarkable Phenomena Seen in Switzerland; and an Optical Phenomenon which Occurs on Viewing of a Crystal or Geometrical Solid," *Philosophical Magazine*, 1 (3rd series), pp. 329–37.

26. Recovery of sight cases are reviewed by M. von Senden, *Space and Sight* (London: Methuen, 1960). In a "Frontiers of Learning Confer-

ence" (Lake Como, Italy, October 15–19, 1967), R. L. Gregory took issue with von Senden's findings; more recent literature should be consulted.

27. For the Ames experiments: *The Ames Demonstrations in Perception*, by William H. Ittelson, together with *An Interpretive Manual* by Adelbert Ames, Jr., with a New Introduction by William H. Ittelson (New York: Hafner, 1968). This includes working diagrams. The Ames trapezoid window should be seen to be believed, and a good film presentation of the illusion is presented by Henry Cantril in "Visual Perception (Horizons of Science)," produced by the U. S. Steel Foundation, and available for rental, among other places, from the Audio-Visual Center, Division of University Extension, Indiana University, Bloomington, Ind. 47405; film #ESC 581. An Ames window kit can be purchased from Edmund Scientific Co., 300 Edscope Building, Barrington, N.J. 08007. See also *Explorations in Transactional Psychology*, ed. Franklin P. Kilpatrick (New York: New York University Press, 1961).

28. Paul Riesman, "The Eskimo Discovery of Man's Place in the Universe," *Sign, Image and Symbol*, ed. Gyorgy Kepes (New York: George Braziller, 1966), pp. 226ff.

29. Reported by Gordon W. Allport and Thomas F. Pettigrew, "Cultural Influences on the Perception of Movement: The Trapezoidal Illusion Among Zulus," *Journal of Abnormal Social Psychology*, 55 (1957), pp. 104–13. Their work is discussed by Marshall H. Segall, Donald T. Campbell, and Melville J. Herskovits, *The Influence of Culture on Visual Perception* (Indianapolis, Ind.: Bobbs-Merrill, 1966), p. 66 and passim.

30. For Marshall McLuhan's ideas, the best source is still his *The Gutenberg Galaxy* (Toronto: Univ. of Toronto Press, 1962).

31. Edward Carpenter, "Image Making in Arctic Art," from *Sign, Image and Symbol* by Gyorgy Kepes, p. 221. Reprinted with permission of the publisher. Copyright © 1966 by Gyorgy Kepes.

32. Ibid., p. 218.

33. Ibid., p. 214.

34. On perspective in art and its relationship to culture, see Erwin Panofsky, *Early Netherlandish Painting* (Cambridge, Mass.: Harvard University Press, 1954) and *Renaissance and Renascences in Western Art* (1960); John White, "Developments in Renaissance Perspective,"

*Journal of the Warburg and Courtauld Institutes*, 12 (1949), pp. 58–79, and 14 (1951), pp. 42–69; William J. Ivins, *Art and Geometry* (Cambridge, Mass.: Harvard University Press, 1946); E. H. Gombrich, *Art and Illusion* (New York: Pantheon, 1960).

35. J. Bagby, "A Cross-Cultural Study of Perceptual Dominance in Binocular Rivalry," *Journal of Abnormal Social Psychology*, 54 (1957), pp. 331–34. A review of such studies is given by Henri Jajfel, *The Handbook of Social Psychology*, Vol. III, ed. Gardner Lindzey and Elliot Aronson (2d ed.; Reading, Mass.: Addison-Wesley, 1969), pp. 369–70.

36. See M. D. Vernon, *The Psychology of Perception* (Baltimore, Md.: Penguin, 1962), chap. 11.

37. Reported by John R. Frederiksen, "Cognitive Factors in the Recognition of Ambiguous Auditory and Visual Stimuli," *Journal of Personal and Social Psychology*, 7 (1967), pp. 1ff.

38. See Edward Engel, "Binocular Methods in Psychological Research," *Explorations in Transactional Psychology*, ed. Franklin P. Kilpatrick (New York: New York University Press, 1970), p. 303.

39. Reported in V. I. Pudovkin, *Film Technique and Film Acting* (London, 1954).

40. A short account is given by Robert Rosenthal in *American Behavioral Scientist*, 10 (1967) and a more extended one in his *Pygmalion in the Classroom* (New York: Holt, Rinehart & Winston, 1968).

## 6. How to Carve Up a Universe: Cognition

1. As one discussion of naming, there is Roger Brown, "How Shall a Thing Be Called?" *Language*, ed. R. C. Oldfield and J. C. Marshall (Baltimore, Md.: Penguin, 1968), pp. 82–91; also Roger Brown, *Words and Things* (Chicago: Free Press, 1958).

2. Jerome S. Bruner and Rose R. Oliver, "Development of Equivalence Transformations in Children," a monograph of the *Society for Research in Child Development*, 28 (1963) (Whole No. 86), pp. 125–41. Reprinted in *Readings in the Psychology of Cognition*, ed. Richard C. Anderson and David P. Ausubel (New York: Holt, Rinehart & Winston, 1966), pp. 415–34.

3. For the object sorting test, see D. Rapaport, M. Gill, and R. Schafer, *Diagnostic Psychological Testing* (Chicago: Year Book Publishers, 1945). It is discussed by Paul W. Pruyser in his *Dynamic Psychology of Religion* (New York: Harper & Row, 1968), pp. 76ff. A paper and

pencil form of the test has been prepared by H. N. Sloane, "The Generality and Construct Validity of Equivalence Range," unpublished doctoral dissertation, on file, Pennsylvania State University library.

4. Donald R. Gorham, "The Proverbs Test," *Psychological Reports*, 2 (1956), Supplement 1, pp. 1–12.

5. On "hesitation," see F. Goldman-Eisler, *Psycholinguistics: Experiments in Spontaneous Speech* (New York: Academic Press, 1968).

6. On language, Eric Lenneberg, "Language and Cognition," *The Biological Foundations of Language* (New York: John Wiley & Sons, 1967), with the appendix by Noam Chomsky; also, J. R. Hayes, ed., *Cognition and the Development of Language* (New York: John Wiley & Sons, 1970). Also useful is *Language in Thinking*, ed. Parven Adams (Baltimore, Md.: Penguin, 1972).

7. Whorf's selected writings have been collected as *Language, Thought and Reality*, ed. John B. Carroll (Cambridge, Mass.: M.I.T. Press, 1956). The literature of the discussion of Whorf is summarized by C. Kluckhohn, "Notes on Some Anthropological Aspects of Communication," *American Anthropologist*, 63 (1961), pp. 896–910.

8. Whorf, op. cit., p. 213.

9. Joshua A. Fishman, "A Systematization of the Whorfian Hypothesis," *Behavioral Science*, 5 (1960), pp. 323–39, reprinted in Alfred G. Smith, ed., *Communication and Culture* (New York: Holt, Rinehart & Winston, 1966), pp. 505–16.

10. Quoted by Fishman, in Smith, op. cit., p. 514. Reproduced by permission of the American Anthropological Association from Memoir 79 of the American Anthropological Association (1954), pp. 106–23. See Charles F. Hockett, *A Course in Modern Linguistics* (New York: Macmillan, 1958).

11. Reported by Leonard Schatzman and Anselm Strauss, "Social Class and Modes of Communication," *American Journal of Sociology*, 60 (1955), pp. 329–38, and reprinted in Smith, op. cit., chap. 42, pp. 442–55.

## 7. Tolerance for Ambiguity: Cognitive Styles

1. A review of studies concerning the nature of attitudes is given by William J. McGuire, "The Nature of Attitudes and Attitude Change," *The Handbook of Social Psychology*, Vol. III, ed. Gardner Lindzey and Elliot Aronson (2d ed.; Reading, Mass.: Addison-Wesley, 1969), chap.

21. See also the useful collection of articles in *Attitudes*, ed. Marie Jahoda and Neil Warren (Baltimore, Md.: Penguin, 1966).

2. Some notes on the history of rigidity studies are given by Penelope Jane Leach in *Thought and Personality*, ed. Peter B. Warr (Baltimore, Md.: Penguin, 1970), pp. 19–35.

3. Else Frenkel-Brunswik, "Intolerance of Ambiguity as an Emotional and Personality Variable," *Journal of Personality*, 18 (1949), p. 108. The work is discussed by M. D. Vernon, *The Psychology of Perception* (Baltimore, Md.: Penguin, 1962), pp. 202ff.

4. Quoted by Leach in Warr, op. cit., p. 29, from *Journal of Personality*, 18 (1949), p. 108.

5. *The Authoritarian Personality*, ed. T. W. Adorno et al. (New York: Harper & Row, 1950), available in a paperback edition. It has been followed by many reviews and studies, especially R. Christie and M. Jahoda, *Studies in the Scope and Method of "The Authoritarian Personality"* (Chicago: Free Press, 1956).

6. Budner's work is reported in *Journal of Personality*, 30 (1962), pp. 29–50.

7. Harvey's work is briefly presented in an article, "Conceptual Systems and Attitude Change," *Attitude, Ego-Involvement and Change*, ed. Carolyn W. Sherif and Muzafer Sherif (New York: John Wiley & Sons, 1968), chap. 11, and more extensively in *Motivation and Social Interaction*, which he edited (New York: Ronald Press, 1963).

8. Harvey in Sherif and Sherif, op. cit., pp. 105–6. Used by permission.

9. An expanded version of these ideas is presented by Harvey in *Motivation and Social Interaction*, p. 116.

10. Milton Rokeach, *The Open and Closed Mind* (New York: Basic Books, 1960). A review of nearly a decade of studies of the Rokeach work was made by Ralph B. Vacchiano, Paul S. Strauss, and Leonard Hockman, "The Open and Closed Mind: A Review of Dogmatism," *The Psychological Bulletin*, 71 (1969), pp. 261–73.

11. Rokeach, *The Open and Closed Mind*, © 1960 by Basic Books, Inc., Publishers, New York, p. 14. Used by permission.

12. Ibid., p. 35.

13. Ibid., pp. 7–8.

14. Ibid., p. 41.

15. Ibid., pp. 69–70.

16. Ibid., p. 67.

17. Ibid., p. 57.

18. Ibid., p. 66.

19. Ibid., pp. 73ff.

20. In Lindzey and Aronson, op. cit., Vol. V, chap. 44.

## 8. Cognitive Tuning: Preaching in a New Key

1. The first edition (1918) was rewritten. A brief account of Barth's "pilgrimage" is given by Arnold B. Come, *An Introduction to Barth's Dogmatics for Preachers* (Philadelphia: Westminster Press, 1963), especially p. 36.

2. From *The Preaching of the Gospel* by Karl Barth, p. 9. Translated by B. E. Hooke. Published in the U.S.A. by The Westminster Press, 1963. English translation © S.C.M. Press, Ltd., 1963. Used by permission.

3. Ibid., p. 16.

4. Nebreda position is given in his book, *Kerygma in Crisis?* (Chicago: Loyola University Press, 1965), and in an article, "The Preparation of the Message," *Lumen Vitae*, 16 (1961), pp. 399–416.

5. The phrase is from Ninian Smart, *Prospect for Metaphysics*, ed. I. T. Ramsey (Westport, Conn.: Greenwood, 1961). I have taken it from the essay by Howard Root, *Soundings*, ed. Alec R. Vidler (New York: Cambridge University Press, 1962), p. 3.

6. Running in parallel with many of these ideas is Fred B. Craddock, *As One Without Authority* (Enid, Okla.: Phillips University Press, 1971), which I have seen too late to incorporate into my own work.

7. Paul Matussek, "The Function of the Sermon with Regard to Repressed Unbelief in the Believer," *The Pastoral Approach to Atheism*, ed. Karl Rahner (Glenrock, N.J.: Paulist Press, 1967), pp. 112–21.

8. Barth, op. cit., p. 17.

9. Susanne K. Langer, *Philosophy in a New Key* (Cambridge, Mass.: Harvard University Press, 1942).

10. Ibid., p. 4. Copyright, 1942, 1951, by the President and Fellows of Harvard College. Used by permission.

11. Ibid., p. 25.

12. Ibid., p. 24.

13. T. Patrick Burke, in *Searching in the Syntax of Things*, ed. Maurice Friedman, T. Patrick Burke, and Samuel Laeuchli (Philadelphia: Fortress Press, 1972), p. 31.

# About the Author

Clement W. Welsh, a native of Oakmont, Pennsylvania, is a graduate of Harvard College, the Episcopal Theological School, and Harvard University (Ph.D.). From 1942–57 he taught at Kenyon College, Gambier, Ohio; was editor of Forward Movement Publications from 1957–63; and since 1963 has been Director of Studies and Warden, College of Preachers, and Canon Theologian, Washington Cathedral.

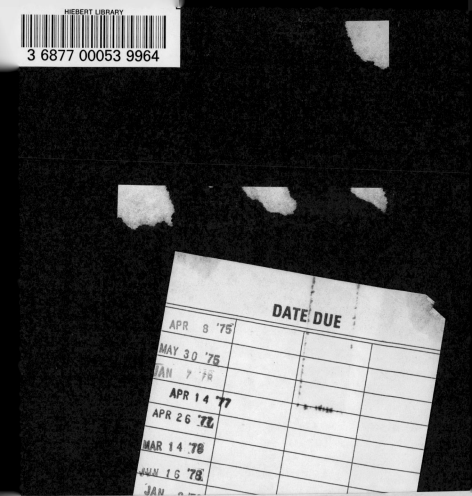

DATE DUE

| APR 8 '75 | | |
|---|---|---|
| MAY 30 '75 | | |
| JAN 7 '76 | | |
| APR 14 77 | | |
| APR 26 '77 | | |
| MAR 14 '78 | | |
| JUN 16 '78 | | |
| JAN | | |

**Welsh, Clement,** 1913–
Preaching in a new key: Studies in the psychology of thinking and listening. Philadelphia, United Church Press [1974]

128 p. 22 cm.

"A Pilgrim Press book."
Includes bibliographical references.

1. Preaching. 2. Perception. 3. Cognition. I. Title.

BV4211.2.W42      251      74–5268
ISBN 0–8298–0273–8      MARC

Library of Congress  74 [4]